THE
PERSONAL
SECURITY
HANDBOOK

THE
PERSONAL
SECURITY
HANDBOOK

DR. CHRIS McNAB and JOANNA RABIGER

The Lyons Press
Guilford, CT 06437
The Lyons Press is an imprint of The Globe Pequot Press

First Lyons Press edition, 2003

The Lyons Press is an imprint of The Globe Pequot Press.

Editorial and design by:
Amber Books Ltd
Bradley's Close
74–77 White Lion Street
London N1 9PF
www.amberbooks.co.uk

Project Editor: Mariano Kälfors
Design: Hawes Design
Illustrations: Tony Randell and Kevin Jones Associates

PICTURE CREDITS
Artworks: Amber Books Ltd

Printed in Italy by Eurolitho S.p.A.

2   4   6   8   10   9   7   5   3   1

The Library of Congress Cataloging-in-Publication Data is available on file.

ISBN 1-58574-831-5

DISCLAIMER

Contents

Resources list

Home Security and Safety

Home Security
Tel 1 800 669 7328
products@securityworld.com
http://www.securityworld.com/

A&E Security
Tel 1 800 889 4471
http://www.aesecurity.com/

Ace Hardware
Tel 630 990 6600
http://www.acehardware.com/

Bosch Security Systems
http://www.boschsecuritysystems
.com/

DSC Security
http://www.dscsec.com/dscindex.
htm

First Alert
Tel 1 800 793 5949
http://www.firstalertpro.com/

IR Security & Safety
Tel 317 613 8944
http://www.irsecurityandsafety.
com/

YSG Door Security Consultants
Tel 1 800 438 1951
http://www.yalesecurity.com/

Fire Prevention and Alarm Systems

Ademco Security
http://www.ademco.com/

Faraday
Tel 517 423 2111
http://www.faradayllc.com/

Gamewell
Tel 1 888-FIREBOX
http://www.gamewell.com/

Silent Knight
Tel 1 800 328 0103
http://www.silentknight.com/

System Sensor
Tel 1 800 736 7672
http://www.systemsensor.com/

Gun Security

Federal Safety Equipment Inc.
Tel 480 899 7340
cdpublicsafety@aol.com
http://www.federal-safety-
equipment.com/

Automobile Security

SecureRite.com
Tel 1 800 241 3930
http://www.securerite.com/

Carlocks.com
Tel 425 556 1900
http://www.carlocks.com/

Motor Traders
http://www.motortraders.com/

Wolo Automobile Products
Tel 1 800 645 5808
http://www.wolo-mfg.com/

Protective Clothing and Equipment

Industrial Safety Company
http://www.indlsafety.com/

Omark Safety Equipment
http://www.omarksafety.com/

Northern Safety.Com
Tel 1 800 631 1246
http://www.northernsafety.com/

American AllSafe Company
Tel 1 800 231 1332
http://www.americanallsafe.com/

Martial Arts and Self-Defense Organizations

The Martial Arts Information Center
http://www.napma.com/

United States Martial Arts Association
http://www.mararts.org/

United States Martial Arts
Federation
http://www.usmaf.org/

American Amateur Karate
Foundation
http://www.aakf.org/

American Judo and Jujitso
Federation
http://www.ajjf.org/

National Women's Martial Arts
Federation
http://nwmaf.org/

Self-defense Equipment

American Martial Arts Supply
http://www.amas.net/

Superfoots.com
http://www.superfoots.com/

World-Wide Martial Arts Supply
http://www.wwmas.com/

Security and Bodyguard Services

American Bodyguard Association
http://www.americanbodyguard.
org/

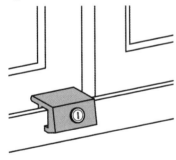

Richard W. Kobetz & Associates, LTD
Executive Protection Institute
http://www.personalprotection.
com/

Advanced Driving & Security Inc.
http://www.1adsi.com/

First-aid Equipment

International First Aid
Tel 1 800 FRST AID
http://www.InternationalFirstAid.
com/

Gutz
Tel 1 888 249 8888
http://www.gutz.com/

Omark Safety Equipment
http://www.omarksafety.com/

Public Safety Information Websites

National Safety Council
http://www.nsc.org/

National Crime Prevention
Council
http://www.ncpc.org/neigh.htm

Federal Bureau of Investigation
http://www.fbi.gov/homepage.htm

United States Department of
Justice
http://www.usdoj.gov/

National Sheriffs' Association
http://www.sheriffs.org/

FirstGov
http://www.firstgov.gov/

National Fire Protection
Association
http://www.nfpa.org/

U.S. Fire Administration
http://www.usfa.fema.gov/

CarbonMonoxideKills.Com
http://www.carbonmonoxidekills.
com/

National Library of Medicine/
National Institutes of Health
http://www.nlm.nih.gov/
medlineplus/

National Neighborhood Watch
Institute
http://www.nnwi.org/

US Environmental Protection
Agency
http://www.epa.gov/iaq/co.html

Advocates for Highway and Auto
Safety
http://www.saferoads.org/

AutoSafety.com
http://www.autosafety.com/

National Highway Traffic Safety
Administration
http://www.nhtsa.dot.gov/cars/

Public Transport Safety
National Security Institute
http://nsi.org/

Federal Aviation Administration
http://www.faa.gov

The Skyrage Foundation
http://www.skyrage.org

Gulf Coast Storm Alert Network
http://www.stormalert.net/

American Red Cross
http://www.redcross.org/

Federal Emergency Management
Agency
http://www.fema.gov/

National Center for Infectious
Diseases
http://www.cdc.gov/ncidod/
diseases/

CHAPTER ONE

Introduction

In spite of recent trends towards inner-city revitalization and gentrification, urban areas continue to suffer far higher rates of homicide, violent crime, and household break-ins than suburban or rural areas.

In recent years, hundreds of acres of former warehouse or housing projects and ghetto neighbourhoods have been converted into prime retail and rental property, and the trend continues in many former industrial cities. Outsiders moving into newly gentrified neighbourhoods often fall prey to hostile and opportunistic attacks, such as car thefts and muggings, and rape. Almost every city dweller has experienced, or will experience, a burglary, an intimidation, or street robbery that has some connection with illegal drug use or with feeding a drug habit.

BIG CITIES BREED ANONYMITY

Cities are subject to a constant traffic of short-term residencies, and fostering a sense of community or neighbourly relations can be challenging. The make-up of any city is diverse, constantly changing, and almost always prone to anonymity. Simply by being populous, cities provide cover for all kinds of people – including those on parole for violent crimes, those with psychiatric problems, and many other volatile or unpredictable types. A crowded bar in a major city or a lonely street can equally prove a source of violence. For this reason, cities are places in which we must be on guard at all times.

A GROWING THREAT

Larger urban areas attract a wide variety of people. The more important cities in the United States and in Europe have all been subjected to terrorist strikes or bombing campaigns by terrorist groups because of their dense populations and the values or political government which they may be

Profile of urban crime

- 8 urban residents per 1000 are victims of an aggravated assault.
- 55 per cent of all robberies are committed using a weapon.
- 7 per cent of all rapes/sexual assaults involve a weapon.

- Urban males are almost half as likely to be violently victimized as urban females.
- Urban residences (46.2) have a higher burglary rate than suburban (27.1) or rural homes (32.6) per 1000 households.

BEING STREETWISE, BEING EMPOWERED

City living demands a state of constant high alert, and a passive or defeatist attitude towards its dangers serves little purpose. However, mentally engaging with the city's darker side can yield a new realism. Developing a game plan for every urban threat can lead to greatly increased confidence in one's daily judgements and practices.

To be truly streetwise requires more than reliance on urban myths: understanding how the city's many dangerous facets function and how to survive them demands more detailed study. This book sets out to warn the reader of every conceivable urban challenge, including the most traumatic scenarios, without seeking to scaremonger or to fuel alarmism, but in order to empower.

seen to represent. Knowing what to do and how to act in the event of a terrorist scare or strike now forms a necessary component of all urban living today worldwide.

NATURE STRIKES

Cities are not exempt from natural disaster either: Los Angeles and San Francisco are both prone to earthquakes, and many other major cities have known tsunamis, tornadoes, hurricanes, and severe flooding. Blizzards can also have a devastating effect, bringing cities such as Buffalo, in the Great Lakes of the United States, to a standstill.

Although city authorities coordinate disaster warnings and evacuation plans, there is much to be gained from preparing for such an event in advance and for having some idea of what to expect. Be sure to study Red Cross advice and to find out what your local emergency plan would entail.

RAISE YOUR AWARENESS

Many of us are deeply attached to the diversity and stimuli of the big city and pride ourselves on our mobility, our lack of neuroses, and the dynamic pace of our lives. We may be prepared to take calculated risks in order fully to enjoy our city, for example, returning home late on an empty subway from a downtown performance or driving through a strange neighbourhood to a

Burglary facts

- A burglary occurs every 3 seconds in the United States.
- On average, 1 out of 6 homes will be burgled every year.
- Half of all burglaries take place without forced entry.

- The average burglar will give up on forced entry after 4 minutes.
- 60 per cent of residential burglaries occur during daylight hours.

- Homes without proper security systems are estimated to be 2.7 times more likely to be targeted by a burglar.
- Nearly 500,000 intrusions will result in bodily injury.

historic sports arena. But with prior planning, awareness, and understanding, we can both be mentally prepared to respond to a menacing situation and sharpen our judgement in the event of a crisis, thereby reducing our overall level of risk and increasing our chances of escaping unhurt.

This book is a practical guide designed to raise awareness by addressing every possible angle of numerous potentially dangerous situations – with an emphasis on understanding the relation between cause and effect, and how best to react and respond. Far from inducing paranoia and fear, you are invited to take control, to behave decisively, and to negotiate urban complexity with increased skill and confidence.

Urban survival begins at home. Without adequate security fittings, an urban home is vulnerable to intrusion, and, if the intruder is apprehended within the property, this can have serious or even fatal consequences. Knowing how to secure your urban home and how to discourage burglars can indeed save lives.

Become streetwise

Be aware of the unwanted attention that your style of dress and belongings may attract, and avoid taking shortcuts through unfamiliar parts of the city.

DANGER IN THE HOME

Crime is not the only killer in cities. Ironically, the place where we generally feel safe – at home – is the very place where we are most at risk. As many as 20,0000 Americans die in accidents at home each year, and an additional 7 million are hurt. The leading cause of death is falls, affecting in particular elderly populations; the second leading cause of death at home is poisoning, including death from inhalation of dangerous

Be aware

Failing to focus on your surroundings only gives opportunists time to study and prepare to take advantage of you. Never reveal valuables, such as a laptop, in public places.

Household fires

- 85 per cent of fire deaths occur in the home.
- 75 per cent of home fire victims die upstairs from downstairs fires.
- Suffocation or asphyxiation causes most fire deaths.
- Approximately 40,000 people die in household fires in the United States every year.
- In Great Britain, 59 per cent of home fires start in the kitchen, 24 per cent from pans of fat or oil.

fumes. An estimated 4000 people a year die in the United States from household fires. About 1500 people die each year from accidental carbon monoxide poisoning, which remains the number-one source of accidental poisoning deaths in the United States.

Death from fire and carbon monoxide poisoning is, however, preventable: only one-fifth of the home fire deaths in the period 1989–98 were caused by fires in which a smoke alarm was present and operated. This book provides comprehensive information for making the home safe for all.

ASSESSING RISKS ON CITY STREETS

On the street, violent assault can result in injuries inflicted by a punch or blow to the head, a slash with a knife or sharp object, or a shooting. For women in cities, sexual assault or rape is a constant and appalling possibility. Any urban citizen stands to learn much from increasing his or her ability to 'read' behaviour in a street context. Understanding how to plot a safe route through a city and those areas to avoid is also key. Knowing when to run and when to fight is, for anyone, regardless of gender, a crucial process.

Learning to defend yourself offers real security and safety benefits, and is widely recommended by the police. For men and women alike, knowing how different parts of the body can be used to deflect an assault and developing mental clarity and concentration while under attack are vital survival skills.

VEHICLE-RELATED CRIME

Cities are notorious for car theft, competitive and aggressive driving, and road traffic accidents. Carjacking is a particularly alarming new crime trend involving the theft or attempted theft of a motor vehicle by force or threat of force. Between

1987 and 1992, carjacking accounted for 2 per cent of the 1.9 million vehicle thefts per year that occurred in the US. Robberies and rapes frequently take place as the victim is getting in or out of his or her car.

Understanding the factors that make you more vulnerable to such an attack and knowing how best to select a parking space are essential to your security and require careful attention to detail and to situation. As well as knowing how to deal with driving-related crime, every driver should have some knowledge of how to cope in a road-traffic accident or if there is a fire in the vehicle. Understanding how to prevent vehicle fires and knowing how to respond to road traffic injuries can save lives.

commuters. In this book you will find a check-list of situations to avoid and ways and means of refining your public transportation awareness skills, so that you can travel defensively.

COMBATING TERRORISM

Since the events of 11 September 2001, the world has been on alert for terrorist strikes and airplane hijacks. Terrorism has plagued much of the world for many years. and the United States' recent awakening to the threat has sparked a mass drive towards public awareness in that country. Using examples drawn from daily life and routines, this guide breaks down the elements of survival into easy-to-understand facts and advice. It

SELF-PROTECTION WHEN TRAVELLING

Travel by subway or light rail is an everyday event for many urban dwellers, but no less dangerous for that reason, particularly when forced to return home late at night. This guide details the precautions you will need to take, particularly those who must travel during antisocial hours or on user-light routes.

Subway platforms in major cities such as New York gained a reputation for crime during the 1980s, and, although much has been done to address this aspect of city living, the isolation of subway spaces means that using public transportation still carries an above-average risk level. Many serious assaults are committed at subway station exits – often poorly lit and isolated – or in adjacent car parks used by

Close to home

Travel awareness should extend to your home, where predators may lurk.

Be alert and take the safest route possible from your parked car to your front door.

Carjacking

Carjacking is usually a highly organized crime in which a valuable car may be stolen at gunpoint. Plan your route carefully, and never stop your car in unfamiliar or lonely parts of the city.

provides guidance on tracking suspicious behaviour, what to look out for in a new age of global terrorist threat, how to react in a bomb threat situation, and how to cope with some of the worst imaginable situations.

SURVIVING NATURAL CALAMITIES

Natural disasters such as hurricanes, tornadoes, flooding, and even periods of heavy snowfall can take on nightmarish proportions when utilities such as water and electricity are cut

and cities are quickly reduced to chaos. The information in this book describes the steps to take to prepare your home for a major natural disaster, the action to take in the event of a natural disaster warning, and how to survive a period of diminished services and power.

BASIC FIRST AID

Lastly, every urban dweller should have some knowledge of first aid. Knowing how to use a first-aid kit is covered in the last chapter,

Carjacking statistics

- About 7 out of 10 completed carjackings involved firearms, compared with 2 out of 10 attempted carjackings.
- About 16 per cent of victims of attempted or completed carjackings were injured. Serious injuries, such as gunshot or knife wounds, broken bones, internal injuries, and loss of consciousness, occurred in about 4 per cent of all carjackings.
- 40 per cent of incidents took place in an open area, away from the victim's home; for example, near a bus, subway, or train station or near an airport; 20 per cent occurred in parking lots or near commercial places, such as shops, restaurants, gas stations, and office buildings.

- Between 1992 and 1996, an average of about 49,000 attempted or completed carjackings occurred in the United States each year.
- Urban residents are considered by the US Department of Justice Bureau of Justice Statistics more likely to experience carjacking than suburban or rural residents.
- A weapon of some type was used in 83 per cent of all carjackings.

The threat of terrorism

After a series of anthrax attacks in the United States, fears of biological warfare can now be justified.

from dealing with heavy bleeding, shock, and cardiac arrest to diagnosing life-threatening conditions. The correct response to severe injuries can save lives.

Urban living is exciting and stimulating at best, and bewildering and dangerous at worst. This book promotes an informed and active attitude to urban living that will considerably enhance our enjoyment and understanding of the complexity and challenges that living in the city today entails.

Home security and safety

We tend to feel comfortable and relaxed inside our homes, and it can be hard to imagine anything going wrong once we have locked the door behind us.

Yet all too often, our seemingly secure homes take as little as 60 seconds to break into; our basements contain flammable or explosive materials, waiting to be triggered; and there are numerous fire hazards around the home of which we are dangerously unaware. Although we may not realize it, we are usually many times more vulnerable to danger than we might think.

Overlooking the necessary preventative measures around the home and garden can have very serious consequences. Knowing how to prevent domestic disasters is as important as knowing how to cope with the outcome when danger strikes. Today burglary is often committed by drug users, and it is more likely than ever before to entail rape, robbery, and assault. Fire is a leading cause of death in the home. And accidents in the home that cause fatal falls are a major cause of death for the elderly.

In order to feel relaxed and safe in the home, we need to think through all the various details of our home's construction and principles of organization. For until we fully understand the principles and specifics that underpin effective deterrence, prevention, and preparedness, our homes could not only fail to protect us, but also be lulling us into a false sense of security.

DOOR SAFETY

The parts of the house most vulnerable to intrusion are the doors and windows. Doors are most intruders' preferred means of accessing the property, as an open door will allow them to make off with larger items. Back doors, often hidden away from the garden by the garden fence or by shrubbery, are broken into more often than front doors.

It can prove alarmingly easy for an intruder to break through a weaker exterior door, and there is almost no point fitting high-security locks to a poor-quality door. Hollow wooden doors are easily kicked in, and a glass panel in a door is easily broken, allowing the intruder to reach through to the inside lock. If glass in a door cannot be replaced, a double cylinder lock preventing it from being opened from the inside is essential. A solid, metal core door without any glass in it is the most secure choice for both front and back doors.

Although a relatively unusual construction practice, the hinges of the front door are sometimes left exposed to the exterior, making it very easy for an intruder to pop them and remove the door altogether. Replacing such hinges with those that use setscrews with non-removable pins improves this situation, but resetting the hinges on the interior of the door is an even surer solution.

The doorframe and doorjambs that form part of the frame are also extremely important. If the door does not fit tightly against the frame, the resulting gap can be pried with a crowbar. A door that has become loose or warped, and no longer fits its frame is a security risk. Similarly, if the doorframe is not sealed to the walls of the home, it, too, can be forced open and the door removed.

Front door security

- Never open the front door to a stranger or unexpected caller.
- Never rely on a key chain for protection.
- If you notice a strange vehicle parked on your street, make a note of the licence plate number.
- If you have seen suspicious-looking strangers sitting inside the vehicle, notify the police.
- If you arrive home to find the door open, never go inside. Call the police from elsewhere.
- Never put a first name on a mailbox. Use initials and last name only.
- Never leave notes indicating you aren't home or when you will return.
- Never attach a name or licence tag to your house keys.
- Never attach a key to the inside door mailbox.
- House numbers should be visible from the street so that police, fire, or medical personnel can more easily respond to a call.

Never open your door and rely on a chain lock to keep a would be assailant out. A keyhole is essential to all homes for identifying any callers.

Cladding the doorframe with metal can provide the necessary additional protection.

Lastly, any good-quality door should be fitted with a viewer or peephole that has a 180-degree viewing area. This will allow a good view of any caller to the house and should be backed up by good exterior doorway illumination. Installing a viewer in the back door as well as the front door is a good additional safety measure.

DOOR LOCKS

A professional armed with only a credit card or a screwdriver can usually open the common key-in-knob lock in a matter of seconds. Most rim locks can also be forced or manipulated. For greatly increased security, every exterior door to the home – including back and side doors and the door leading to the garage – should be fitted with a good-quality deadlock.

A deadlock is a mortise lock, controlled by a key. A mortise is a slot or hole cut into the edge of a door into which a lock or latch is slotted. Mortise deadlocks are the most secure mechanical locks available because, once extended, the bolt locks into position and cannot be forced back without use of a key. By contrast, a spring-loaded latch can be manipulated by use of force.

Deadlock bolts give greater protection

For maximum security, the deadlock bolt should be at least 2.5cm (1in) of solid metal (preferably steel) and should have a rotating steel pin within the bolt in order to make it hacksaw-resistant. It should ideally feature a free-spinning brass cover over the outside cylinder, in order to be wrench-resistant. The keyway should contain a five-pin tumbler system to make picking the lock more

Deadbolt lock

Deadbolt locks are the most secure and are relatively easy to fit yourself using a drill and templates provided by the manufacturer.

difficult. The connecting screws in the lock should be steel. Screw heads should not be exposed on the outside.

Lock-use precautions

A double-cylinder, double-keyed lock can be locked on the way out and cannot be opened from the inside without a key. This is the only kind of lock that should ever be used in conjunction with glass in the door, to prevent smash and grab. This lock also

Door construction essentials

- Use solid wood or metal core.
- Avoid glass panels.
- Two locks are always better than one.
- Hinges should never be exposed to the exterior.
- Use long screws in the door

frame – at least 7.5cm (3in).
- When buying replacement doors, buy with the surround to ensure accurate fit.
- Metal stripping around the doorjamb can make the doorframe less vulnerable.

Door lock essentials

- Mortise deadlocks are the only truly tamper-proof mechanical lock.
- Deadlocks should be made of hacksaw- and wrench-proof materials.
- The deadbolt should extend at least 2.5cm (1in) into the doorframe.
- In glass-panelled doors, a double-cylinder deadbolt lock is essential.
- Internal rack bolts at the top and bottom of the door provide additional security at night.

prevents burglars walking out of the house with large items. However, the drawback of this kind of lock is that, in the event of a fire, occupants in the home could easily be trapped inside if overwhelmed by smoke and unable to reach for or locate the key.

One way around this would be to use this lock only when all occupants of the house have left the premises and, when indoors, to use only the cylinder that prevents access from the outside. In short, to avoid locking occupants inside, use the double cylinder only at times when all occupants have left the house.

The strike plate of a lock is almost as important as the lock itself. Should the strike plate fail to be adequately screwed to the doorframe, it could easily be kicked away. To prevent this, a heavy-duty strike plate should be installed using 7.5cm (3in) wood screws that penetrate deep into the doorframe stud, making it super secure.

Extra bolts

While the main lock on the exterior door should be a deadbolt, adding back-up bolts, in order to give the door more resistance to being kicked in from the outside, is well worthwhile. At night, bolts installed at the top and bottom of the door offer excellent additional security because they cannot be tampered with from the outside. Special impeding door jams that can be wedged in the bottom of the door are also available. Best of all is a rim-mounted lock or vertical deadbolt, mounted to the interior surface of the door and therefore resistant to prying from the outside.

All such locks should be easily operable by occupants inside in the event of a fire. For the same reason, security bars should only be installed if they have a quick-release mechanism. Homeowners and landlords are advised to replace any existing security bars with the quick-release version.

Fitting door locks

Lock mechanisms come in standard sizing and are fitted by boring holes into the door and using good-quality screws. A new lock should never be fitted over the place of the

Hinge bolts

Fitting hinge bolts to your door to reinforce the hinges is relatively easy to do, and they can be found in any hardware store.

former lock, as the wood is usually too chewed up and worn to make a secure holding base. When replacing locks, it is extremely important that you follow the sizing accurately and ensure that the fitting is not loose or unstable. You can usually achieve a tighter fitting of a bolt by using fillers or studs sold in hardware stores. The best solution, however, is to replace the faulty door with a high-security version complete with the most secure locks available.

Precision fitting

The most important point when fitting a new door lock is to follow the template guidelines very carefully in order to coordinate the relation between the two holes you will drill – one through the door face for the lock or deadbolt, and the other through the edge of the door for the bolt or latch. In order for the lock to work correctly, these holes must be accurately lined up, so absolute precision is essential. The template provided with the lock is usually a small piece of paper that wraps around the edge of the door in order to indicate where the holes will be located. Mark each place with a sharp instrument or a small nail before you drill.

High-tech door security systems

Although good-quality, well-fitted mechanical locks are highly secure, electronic models are becoming increasingly popular and are decreasing in price. Fingerprint recognition locks have recently become more reliable and are now able to integrate numerous features, including electronic access control. Only a skilled professional should fit electronic and digital security systems.

SECURING PATIO DOORS

Patio doors are extremely vulnerable to break-ins and should always be fitted with additional security devices.

Patio doors should be made of high-impact PVCu and must consist of fully welded joints and a steel reinforced outer frame and opening sash. As well as having secure, anti-tamper deadbolt cylinder locks both at the top and at the bottom of the closing section, the middle section of the patio door – where one piece of glass would in use slide past the other – should be fitted with pin locks that can be unscrewed when the door is in use. In addition to this, an anti-lift device that obstructs the tracks of the patio door is essential. This could be a simple block of wood jammed in the door slide or a specially manufactured 'charley lock'.

Another way of stabilizing a patio door against an intruder is to fit it with a security bar, sometimes known as a 'window jammer'. This is usually a special bar that fits inside the glass horizontally, to give additional reinforcement. Look for a security bar with a patented locking device that can withstand up to 450kg (100lb) of force. The best patio bars are made of steel and prevent the door from opening or being lifted. Patio security bars cannot be dislodged and removed from the outside.

Patio doors allow a potential intruder a panoramic view of the contents of your home and also allow the intruder to see you and your movements. For this reason, be careful to keep desirable electronic items from view, and be mindful that you yourself could be watched while in range of the patio door. Illuminate your home interior in such a way that valuables are not accented. Ideally, your patio doors should be connected to a

Alternatives to mechanical locks

- Card and digital keypad readers
- Digital keypads
- Electric or magnetic door strikes
- Electric doorknob

Window lock

Rather than relying on a window lever that could easily be dislodged to gain entrance, install a window lock which allows windows to be secured with a key.

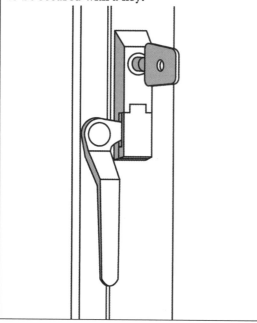

Patio door lock

Locks should be fitted at both the top and bottom of patio doors, or sliding door jams used, to prevent doors being prised open with a crowbar or forced off runners.

home security system and fitted with sensor detectors that trigger an alarm as soon as the patio door is dislodged.

WINDOW SECURITY

As glass can always be broken, it is much harder to secure windows than it is doors. Window glass can be replaced with tempered glass or polycarbonate, but this is costly. The best way of maintaining window security is to keep them locked at all times or to fit them with locks that allow them to be locked when slightly ajar. Downstairs windows are the most vulnerable and should be locked at all times. It is also a good idea to lock upstairs windows, just as you would a front door or downstairs windows, when you leave the house.

Replacing old locks

Older locks on windows are unreliable. By merely inserting a spatula, or flat knife, between the two windows, for example, clasp locks can be easily opened. For this reason, older-style locks that can be easily jimmied or pried should immediately be replaced with a tamper-proof modern version. At best, a secure lock on the window will force the intruder to break the glass, drawing unwanted attention and delaying entry to the house. The more commotion caused, the more likely someone close by is likely to notice.

Securing sash windows

The most common type of window is the double-hung or sash frame window. This type is extremely easy to pry open, and for this reason double-hung windows should ideally be fitted with a steel 4-point deadbolt system that tightly secures the bottom of the top sash to the top of the bottom sash. Pin locks can also be used in a hole bored through the bottom of the top sash window and aligned in a hole in the top of the bottom sash window, allowing both windows to be tightly joined.

Preventing entry through sliding windows

Sliding windows should be treated in the same way as sliding patio doors, that is, with a pin and a jam in the slide track to prevent sliding open. Casement windows are generally the most secure type of window, as long as they are fitted with secure strong and tightly fitting latches. Casement window levers can be locked with a pin lock to the window frame for additional security. Casement windows with cranks can be secured simply by removing the handle, as long as it is left in an accessible place in case of fire.

Vulnerable windows

Jalousie and awning-type windows are the least secure windows because individual panes are easy to pry open or remove. This sort of window should either be replaced or reinforced with bars.

Basement windows should remain permanently locked and fitted with bars, preferably of the kind with a quick-release mechanism, in case of fire.

Security bars on other windows pose too great a potential trap, in the event of a fire, to be worth risking. A better solution is to ensure that all windows are connected to a central alarm system. Battery-operated alarm locks are also available for windows.

A major consideration often overlooked in home security assessment is the window air conditioner, which, in many cases, is easily removed by a burglar, allowing easy access to the home. Air conditioners should be bolted to the house in such a way that they cannot be removed from the outside and the window cannot be raised.

ALARM SYSTEMS

As important as good-quality locks on doors and windows may be, ideally every home should be fitted with an alarm system.

The main components of the home alarm system are:

The control panel

The 'brains' of the security system. The control panel is housed in a protective metal box hidden from sight (for example, in a closet or cupboard). Most alarm panels have an emergency panic button which is linked to the alarm monitoring company and alerts them to call the police.

Three protection zones

The perimeter, interior protection, and entry/exit doors. Each zone is linked to the control panel and will trigger the alarm if disturbed. Perimeter protection is the first area to defend and usually covers the basement, the first floor, and the garage. Interior protection usually consists of motion detectors covering, for example, the first floor and the basement.

The entry/exit zone usually features a delay device, allowing you to enter and exit the premises without setting off the system.

Security keypads

Allow occupants to operate the system by using secret codes and to monitor whether the alarm is on or off. The keypad should be located close to the main entrance/exit point.

Magnetic contacts

Magnets are attached to the door, with a switch on the doorframe so that, when the door is opened, the connection is broken, triggering the alarm. Glass break sensors are attuned to the acoustic shock wave of breaking glass, which also serves to trigger the system.

Sirens (interior and exterior)

The loud alarm that alerts occupants to an intrusion. The exterior siren – mounted in a steel box on an outside wall under the eaves where it cannot be easily tampered with – alerts people nearby and local police.

Alarm systems can be set to protect the home when occupants are absent and to go

Home burglar alarm system

Burglar alarms are the optimal security device for protecting the home. Most alarm systems are set up to trigger a call to a security company and the police in the event of a break-in.

Perimeter sensors

External alarms

Control panel

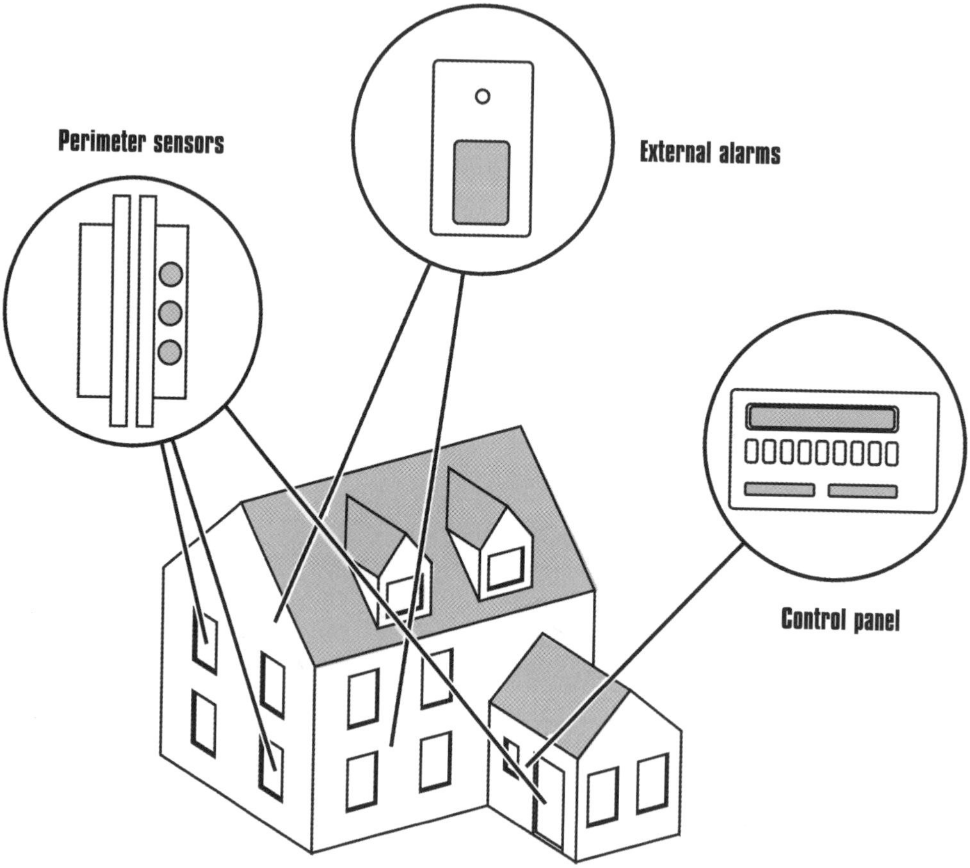

off upon unauthorized entry. Most alarm systems will be wired remotely to contact the alarm company or security agency that will call the police on your behalf in the event of a break-in. The signs that alarm companies provide to display on the lawn or in the window are in themselves an excellent deterrent to potential intruders.

LIGHT UP DARK NOOKS

Shadowy areas around the house will allow predators to lurk unseen in bushes and shrubbery. The home exterior should be lit along walkways, steps, and at the front door. Most importantly, the keyholes to the front and back doors should be well illuminated. Vulnerable parts of the house such as the downstairs windows, sliding doors, and the garage entry door should always be lit at night as a deterrent to intruders.

Set timer lights

It is possible to foil intruders by setting automatic lights within the house that operate even when occupants are absent, using a timer or a photocell. Timers work by setting and must be reset after an electricity cut; however, photocells react to natural light only and turn on at nightfall and off at daybreak. Standard incandescent lights mounted on a

wall or tree are an effective and cost-effective solution. Energy-efficient high-pressure sodium lights or mercury vapour lights are slightly more challenging to maintain, but also offer powerful illumination.

Extra eyes and ears

Security lighting should be chosen for the greatest ease of control. Motion-sensing lights automatically turn on when anything moves within range of the sensor and are perhaps easiest of all. Some detectors work by triggering an alarm when changes in

Hiding places

The predator-proof door on the left is brightly illuminated and free of shadowy hiding places. The door on the right, however, is a safety hazard because a predator could easily hide in the foliage after dark without being detected.

infrared energy levels are sensed as an intruder moves into a protected area, for example, the shrubbery below a downstairs window. In these ways, sensors provide extra eyes and ears around the property and help to cover larger areas.

Equally easy to operate, but dependent upon your operation and presence, remote lighting can be switched on inside the house or from the car as you pull up outside the house or into the driveway.

Lighting to outsmart a burglar

Interior lighting can also be set to automatic timers, and you can vary the lights that are set. Giving the impression that someone is in the house when in fact the home is empty is a good deterrence principle and can be further enhanced by leaving a radio on or setting it to a timer. Soft, low lights that do not reveal the entire room, but suggest that someone is home, perhaps reading in an armchair, achieve the best effect. Avoid illuminating valuables in display cases or setting valuables near windows. Interior illumination should never make a home transparent to the world outside; use blinds or other forms of window fittings to soften and blur the view into the home from outside.

SECURITY IN THE GARDEN

The main principle in garden security is to make it as difficult as possible for intruders to approach or get close to downstairs windows and vulnerable points of entry to the home. There should be limited access to the garden from the street. Garage and shed doors, as well as gate latches, should be fitted with pin-tumbler, laminated rustproof padlocks. While fences may not necessarily prevent an intruder from scaling them, it is far better to have fences than not because the more effort and noise an intruder is forced to undertake, the more he will be deterred from trying.

Good lighting – an effective deterrent

The key factor in garden security is illumination. Lighting should cover the entire front of the house and all hiding places. To make it harder for an intruder to hide, keep shrubbery trimmed and light up or rearrange any dark recesses. Ground cover in the garden should give occupants as much warning as possible of footsteps outside. Use

Lock your shed

The tools inside this shed could be used in a home break-in. Always remember to put tools away after use in the garden and lock your shed securely.

Garden security tips

- Never leave a ladder outside your home.
- Cut off any tree branches that extend to your upstairs windows.
- Avoid creating shadows and hiding places in your garden.
- Keep tools secure.
- Never hide your keys outdoors.
- Always lock gate, garage, shed, and storage warehouse doors.

materials such as small-gauge granite rock that makes noise as you walk on it.

Prevent access to upstairs windows

There should be no way up to the second floor of the house. Any accessible roofs leading to a second-floor window should be wired to the alarm system and covered in noisy gravel. Check the exterior of the house for anything that could be used for scaling the walls, for example, a sturdy vine growing up the side of the house, stacked crates, or the proximity of an outhouse or garden shed.

PLANNING AND CONSTRUCTING A SAFE ROOM

A safe room is a hideaway within the house to which occupants can quickly withdraw in order to call for help in the event of a break-in. Typically, a safe room is created from a master bedroom. It should have a solid, ideally metal-core door and a strong double-cylinder deadlock on the door that locks instantly from the inside (the key can be stored in the master bedroom). A cellular (mobile) phone to call for help should be kept in the safe room at all times, fully charged, as well as a landline phone, set to automatic emergency police dial. Also, keep a fire extinguisher and a first-aid kit in the safe room in case any family member is injured in an attempt to escape. A safe room will need to be well ventilated, in case you and your family are forced to remain there for some time.

Trim branches

Prevent access to upper levels by trimming back tree branches to make them difficult to climb. Strong vines growing up walls may also enable burglars to break in, so be aware of this potential problem too.

TRAINING A GUARD DOG

A dog barking fiercely, heard through a fence or door, is one of the surest deterrents against home intruders. However, owning a security dog is a serious responsibility. A potentially dangerous dog is not the goal; instead, a dog that is easily controlled by you, with a natural territorial instinct and loud bark, is the aim. Certain breeds are better suited to security purposes than others because they have stronger territorial instincts and will bark repeatedly. You should always buy a puppy from a reputable breeder. Be sure to socialize the dog with

Suitable security dog breeds

- Bull mastiff
- Rottweiler
- German shepherd
- Doberman pinscher
- Chow
- Rhodesian ridgeback

Security dogs

Certain breeds have a built-in instinct for guarding the home. The bark of a larger dog is one of the most effective burglar deterrents for the home.

humans and other dogs from an early age. With the help of professional training, your puppy should grow into a manageable, obedient dog.

Dogs bred for guarding property are often very independent and need special training. Training without the assistance, observations and advice of a professional dog trainer is dangerous and should never be attempted. Breeds that are suitable for security or protection are prone to a highly developed self-preservation instinct and for this reason may attack if they think they are being confronted. They are also much less tolerant than other breeds of teasing or abusive treatment and are much more likely to 'turn' on you unless you approach them correctly. For this reason, security dogs should never be left unsupervised with children and are not suitable as family dogs.

All friends and relatives must be briefed never to come by unannounced, and likewise workers who need to come to the house and other strangers will have to be warned of the dog's temperament.

NEIGHBOURHOOD SECURITY PROJECTS

Neighbourhood cooperation is recognized by police as one of the best ways of deterring crime, and it is now widely encouraged as a community-driven crime reduction measure. If a neighbourhood watch scheme already exists, try to attend their regular meetings. If your building or street lacks a neighbourhood watch scheme, contact your local police for advice on setting one up.

Get to know your neighbours

In order to maximize scope, neighbourhood watch schemes should aim to involve all members of the community, from teens to the elderly. Encouraging teenagers to participate in crime prevention is particularly important, as they may be uniquely aware of developing situations in the neighbourhood. Involving teenagers can also help to protect them from any local criminal element.

Involve the whole community

Neighbourhood watch groups must also break down cultural boundaries if they are to succeed. This may entail some multilingual flexibility and translating printed matter into the relevant languages. Successful neighbourhood watch groups should not assume that crime prevention is in the interest of a tiny majority, but should extend their reach throughout the community to immigrant and ethnic minority groups, using churches, other religious organizations, schools, outdoor get-togethers, and casual buffet-style dinners.

Some neighbourhood watch groups use patrols of unarmed volunteers from the neighbourhood to survey the area for signs of criminal activity and report back to the

Ask a neighbour

When you go away on vacation, ask one of your neighbours to remove and store your piled-up mail and newspapers which could attract burglars to your home.

police. Others may simply rely on neighbours' more casual observations and on the exchange of information between them.

The keys to the success of neighbourhood watch schemes lie with the group's ability to delegate tasks, to communicate clearly and efficiently, to set goals, and to act on feedback. Regular meetings, partnerships with other organizations such as a tenants' association or housing authority, consultation

Cultivating a safe neighbourhood

- Get to know all your adjacent neighbours.
- Initiate and reciprocate kind actions.
- Communicate often, and be aware of each other's vacation plans.
- While neighbours are away on vacation, pick up their newspapers and flyers.

Forming a neighbourhood watch

- Get together a small planning committee of neighbours and begin sketching out needs and goals.
- Contact the local police and invite a law enforcement officer to attend your next meeting.
- Publicize your meeting, giving advance notice with door-to-door flyers, and follow up with phone calls the day before.
- Select a meeting place that is accessible to everybody.
- Progressively identify issues that need to be addressed. Invite feedback.
- Elect a chairperson.
- Elect coordinators for each block.
- Establish a list of telephone numbers and e-mail addresses.
- Make a neighbourhood map showing names, addresses, and phone numbers of participating households and distribute to members.

with local police and businesses, information sharing, and aiming to involve everyone – young and old, single and married, renter and homeowner – will all promote the best kind of community effort. Addressing neighbourhood beautification – planting, removing, organizing clean-ups – and encouraging all to light up their homes at night further helps to make your neighbourhood a safer place to live.

RESPONDING TO INTRUDERS

Treat intruders with the greatest caution, and and never attempt a vigilante-style response. Aiming to attack, disarm, or trap an intruder is extremely dangerous and could result in injury or death. Getting away from the property promptly is the safest option.

You should never enter a property that has been broken into before the police have checked it over, so it is vital to recognize the signs of an intrusion when returning to your property, perhaps late at night. If you see a slashed screen, a broken window, or an open door, call the police from a neighbour's house or a public phone. Remain inside your neighbour's house or keep at a safe distance until police help is at hand. Never enter your property until police have inspected it.

What if you hear an intruder?

If you are home and you think you hear someone breaking in, leave your home safely if you can, alerting other family members if possible, then call the police as soon as possible from a safe distance or a neighbour's home. If it is impossible to leave, try to move into a room with a lock and a phone, and call the police. If you are home and an intruder wakes you by breaking into your home, try to get away as quickly and quietly as possible, and go to a safe place before calling the police. You will need to move very quietly, creeping

Apartment building security checklist

- Does your building have a secure admittance system? Is there any control over who enters and leaves the building?
- Are fire stairs locked from the stairwell side above the ground floor, so that you can exit, but no one can enter?
- Are walkways, entrances, parking areas, elevators, hallways, stairways, laundry rooms, and storage areas well lit 24 hours a day?
- Are the mailboxes equipped with quality locks and sited in a public, well-lit area?
- Does the building complex management have a good record on maintenance – for example, do they replace burnt-out lights promptly?

out of the house via the back door or a window. You should never return to the property, even with a group of neighbours, or attempt to confront the intruders or block their escape route.

What if you are confronted?

If the intruder blocks your exit or confronts you, it is very important to stay calm and to avoid acting impulsively. Think about where the nearest phone is and how you might get to it either to press the police touch button or to dial the local police number. Evaluate the situation and look for a chance to escape. You might tell the intruder that all you want to do is leave the house. If they threaten you, this may be the moment to make a noise in order to attract help. One of the best ways of doing this is to smash the window closest to your neighbour's house loudly, in order to alert them to trouble.

PREVENTING DOMESTIC FIRES

The risk of a fire in the home is all too real. While the leading cause of domestic fires is smoking, faulty electrics and cooking are also major contributing factors, and, although modern furniture is manufactured to be moderately fireproof, the average bed or sofa is highly flammable and will quickly give off toxic fumes once it has caught fire. Prevention is essential in order to avoid the all-too-often tragic consequences of a fire in the home.

Fit smoke detectors

It is estimated that more than 40 per cent of residential fires and 60 per cent of residential fatalities occur in homes that have no smoke alarms. For this reason, it is essential to install a smoke

Responding to an intrusion

- Leave the property as soon as you can.
- Call the police at the earliest opportunity.
- If you are trapped indoors, cooperate with the intruder – it may give you the time you need to devise a means of escape.
- Try to make mental note of the intruder's height and appearance, and voice.
- Write down everything you can remember about the intruder afterwards.

detector at every level of your home and near the bedrooms. A smoke detector can be purchased from any hardware store or supermarket. Detectors must be checked once a month, and, if they are battery operated, the batteries must be changed at least once a year, to ensure that the detector works properly. Most detectors will signal when battery power is running low by sounding the alarm. Smoke alarms themselves should be replaced after 10 years of service, or as recommended by the manufacturer.

Heaters

Be aware of your heaters' proximity to waste paper, curtains, and other flammable materials in the house. Always unplug heaters before you go to sleep.

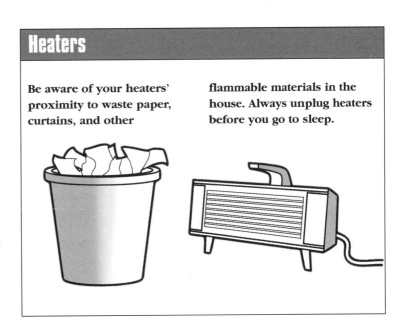

Smoke alarms

Smoke alarms should be installed on the ceiling on every level of your home and particularly outside bedrooms, in order to alert sleeping occupants if there should be a fire. Replace the alarms' batteries regularly according to manufacturers' guidelines.

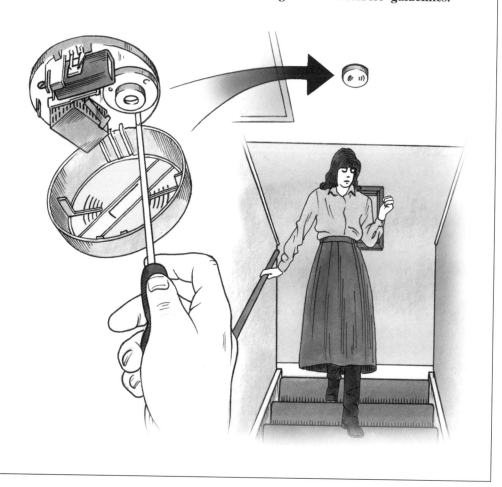

Fire hazards in the home

Home electrical fires are caused by overloading electrical appliances or extension cords, and by misuse and poor maintenance of electrical appliances. Fire deaths are highest during the winter when the use of heating appliances increases. In most cases, faulty electrical wiring causes fires to start in the bedroom. The appliances most likely to cause electrical fires are electric stoves and ovens, dryers, central heating units, televisions, radios, and record or CD players.

Check appliances regularly

Replace older, potentially faulty heaters with new ones wherever possible and have a professional check all heating systems and appliances annually. Heating appliances should be treated with the greatest caution. They should never be placed less than 1m (3ft) away from flammable items such as clothing or paper, or curtains. Fireplace chimneys should be cleaned annually to avoid a chimney fire. Gasoline or camp-stove fuel should never be used indoors.

Consult an electrician if at all in doubt about your electrical circuit load, and keep electrical plugs free from clutter, such as wastepaper trash, which could ignite if surrounding a hot plug or outlet. Do not place cords and wires under rugs, over nails, or in high-traffic areas. Immediately shut off and unplug appliances that sputter, spark, or emit an unusual smell and have them professionally repaired or replaced.

Escaping from a house

Every home should have a fire extinguisher stored in an easily accessible place. This could be just inside the front or back door. Positioning the extinguisher close to a door is a good idea because it can be used close to the door as a point of retreat from the flames and smoke.

A sturdy ladder that can be slung out of a window for escape is also a good emergency tool that can be kept upstairs. Safety sprinklers are another option and one that has become increasingly

Stove tops

Never leave flammable items, such as greaseproof (waxed) paper, on top or close to the cooking range. Never leave food cooking on top of the stove unattended.

Fire prevention essentials

- All electrical wiring should be routinely checked.
- Immediately replace frayed, worn, or damaged appliance electrical cords.
- Never overload extension cords.
- Keep electrical appliances away from wet floors and counters.
- Use three-pronged electrical plugs in three-slot outlets only – never force them into a two-slot outlet.
- Switches that are hot to the touch causing the light to flicker should be switched off immediately and replaced by a professional electrician.
- Replace any electrical tool that gives off shocks or smoke, or smells of burning when used.
- Never smoke in bed.
- Throw out all mattresses made before the early 1970s.
- Buy bedding and furniture that will not burn invisibly whenever possible.
- Never place a heater close to the bedclothes or allow a curtain to drape over it.
- Use lab-approved electrical blankets and regularly check for fraying cords.
- Never leave cooking unattended.
- Keep kitchen materials such as greaseproof (waxed) paper well away from the cooking area.
- Lock matches and lighters away from children.
- Keep heaters well away from flammable objects at all times.

affordable and can offer protection in the event of a fire.

Every occupant in the home should know their escape route, planned from where they sleep, and testing out these escape routes in a family fire drill will maximize your preparedness should there be an emergency.

Storing hazardous substances/materials

Household hazardous materials are common everyday products that are sold in every local supermarket. Yet their potential for danger is great: the top causes of death in the home today are solid and liquid poisonings, falls, fires and burns, and suffocation by ingested objects. Using potentially hazardous substances for heavy-duty cleaning or home improvement may be a necessary evil. But avoiding hazardous materials by using substitutes such as water-based paints or a solution of baking soda and vinegar is a viable alternative.

The following are four major kinds of hazardous materials found in the home:

Corrosive or caustic materials

These are dangerous to the skin and eyes, and can, over time, dissolve a container. Examples of corrosive or caustic materials include:
Metal cleaners with phosphoric acid
Drain cleaners that contain sulphuric acid
Drain cleaners containing sodium hydroxide or lye
Rust removers with hydrofluoric acid
Pool-cleaning chemicals
Ammonia
Bleach

Flammable materials

Flammable items must never be stored near a heat source and should be kept in a cool, dry place. Any exposure to a heat source could result in fire. Most flammable materials are harmful to the skin and the eyes.
Paint
Wood finishes
Thinners
Solvents
Gasoline/petrol
Vehicle-cleaning agents

Explosive or reactive materials

Certain materials, when mixed together, can react in explosive or violent ways. For example, mixing bleach and many dish

Hazardous materials

Protect the labels on bottles and containers from wear and tear, fading, and falling off, so that you are always able to correctly identify the substances within.

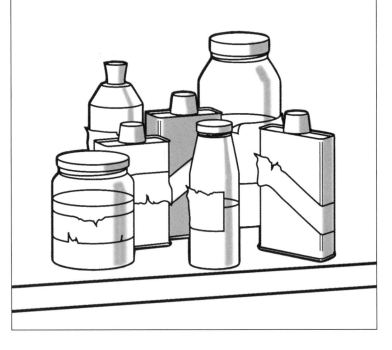

detergents that contain chlorine bleach with ammonia, lye, or acids can produce toxic gases. Some substances will produce toxic gases if exposed to heat, air, or water.

Toxic materials

Usually identified with the symbol of skull and crossbones, toxic materials can cause illness or death. More commonplace toxic materials include pesticides and insecticides, which should always be used in accordance with safety instructions on the label.

Essential precautions in the home

The first principle in storing hazardous materials is to buy as little as possible for each job necessary. Never buy in bulk, and avoid building up a large supply of leftovers.

The second main principle is to avoid storing hazardous materials inside the home. Storing these materials in a secure, locked and well-ventilated outhouse is much safer than storing them indoors. In the event of a fire in the house, or in the event of an earthquake, hazardous materials could ignite and explode, or cause a fire to rage out of control. Leaks inside the home are also of far greater risk to occupants than if they occur in an outhouse.

Outdoor storage sites must be watertight, rodent-proof, and child tamper-proof. If using an outhouse is not possible, building an add-

Fire extinguisher

Place a fire extinguisher close to your back door so that, in the event of a fire, you can use it as you retreat from the house.

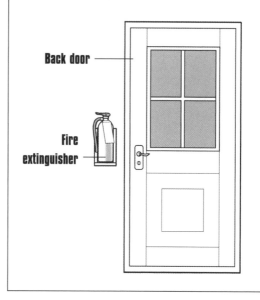

Back door

Fire extinguisher

on storage area to the house or using an explosion-proof metal storage cabinet in the basement is an alternative. Any hazardous materials should be positioned so that they are stable, do not leak, and cannot fall or be easily knocked over.

Hazardous materials dos and don'ts

- Store hazardous materials outside your living space.
- Read all storage instructions on the container.
- Use only approved safety containers for gasoline and solvents.
- Store all containers on low shelves to minimize any possibility of breakage.
- Secure stored containers to minimize breakage further.
- Store containers in a sturdy box or crate to minimize crushing or breaking of containers.
- Store all hazardous materials away from any source of flames, sparks, or hot surfaces.
- NEVER mix acid and chlorine products or store them close to each other, as deadly fumes can result.

The third fundamental is always to store materials in their original containers, making sure to retain the original label and packaging. If a label begins to peel off, do not throw it away; instead, reattach it with transparent tape. Never transfer or store chemical products in household containers such as soda cans/bottles, drinking glasses, and so on. Never reuse empty containers. Always keep containers tightly closed when not in use, and it is vital to keep hazardous materials away from children and pets.

Never store pressurized containers (such as aerosols) in direct sunlight or anywhere that they may come into contact with heat sources – for example, in a car's glove box. Equally to be avoided is storing pressurized containers in damp areas; the weaker a can becomes with rust, the more likely it is to rupture or leak. In a basement, it is a wise precaution to keep hazardous materials stored above potential high-water levels in case of a flood.

Keep a bag of cat litter, sand, or sawdust near to where hazardous materials are stored in order to soak up any spilled chemicals from a broken or leaking container. Never use regular household cleaning items, such as your broom or dustpan, to clean up hazardous materials, as you may inadvertently spread toxic chemicals around the house. Safely dispose of all materials used in cleaning up, and use a special broom for tidying around the cans when in storage. Thoroughly wash all measuring utensils and containers after using hazardous materials, and store these out of reach of children.

MAKING THE HOME SAFE FOR THE ELDERLY OR DISABLED

Falls are the number-one cause of injury-related death for males aged 80 and older, and for females aged 75 and older. One-quarter of those who sustain a hip fracture die within one year, and another 50 per cent never return to their former levels of mobility or independence. Hence preventing a potentially fatal bone-breaking fall is absolutely essential.

Avoid slippery surfaces

Stairs are a major cause of falls. A non-slip ramp may be desirable, in order to access the house safely. A bag of salt should be kept near the front door in cold weather in order to melt snow and ice. Indoors, level and clear floorways are essential. Slippery waxed floors should be avoided. Linoleum can become extremely slippery with wear and should be replaced. Evenly fitted carpeting throughout will protect an elderly or disabled person from hard flooring underneath, but deep pile should be avoided as it makes walking with a frame problematic. Kitchen flooring should be especially flat, without bumps or cracks, or loose pieces of flooring on which feet or a stick might catch. Reduce the number of pieces of small furniture, rugs, and other items that hamper movement.

Easy-to-open doors

Being able to open doors without having to apply pressure or lean on them is very important. No door should be heavy, or jam and need to be forced. All locks and hinges should be oiled to make doors easy to use. Rugs should not block doorways. If the occupant experiences difficulty turning doorknobs, these should be replaced with lever handles.

All living areas, particularly the kitchen, should be well lit. Loose, hanging, or long sections of electricity cords or extensions cords should be avoided by running them securely along walls or floors. Lighting should be easy to switch on and off. Portable telephones are better than those with trailing cords.

Stairs should always have secure handrails that provide sufficient support. Additional handrails and grip bars can be installed on the wall side of stairways for increased stability.

Care in the bathroom

For the elderly or disabled, the bathroom can prove one of the most dangerous rooms in the house. The bathroom should be clear of rugs that might trip; alternatively, fit them with adhesive grips. Carpeting the bathroom is the safest measure. Accidents occurring on the smooth surfaces of the shower or tub are very common, particularly as soap can make surfaces extremely slippery. Traction mats in the bath or shower should always be used. Grip bars should be carefully installed with attention to height and strength. A specialist should also install them in order to ensure that they will resist the weight of a falling adult. If faucets are difficult to turn, replace them with lever handles. Electrical items should never be used in the bathroom.

Kitchen watchpoints

In the kitchen, pots and pans should be stored in an easy-to-reach place, and the number of items should be minimized to avoid accidents caused by searching through cluttered cupboards. No elderly person should be encouraged to use a stepladder, and for this reason all essential daily items should be stored within easy reach. In particular, heavy objects should never be stored on high shelves, as they could

Prevent falls

Store heavy items on low shelves or within easy reach. A safe, sturdy set of steps can be used for occasional climbing, but never use a kitchen stool or chair instead.

Home safety for the elderly and disabled

- The floor must be clear and clutter-free, and telephone and electrical cords kept out of walkways.
- Floors should be unwaxed and any spillages of slippery substance such as cooking oil cleaned up immediately.
- Only non-skid throw rugs

should be used.
- Handrails and grab bars should be fitted in the bathroom.
- All living areas should be well lit.
- Climbing to reach high places should be avoided altogether.

topple off and cause injury. Greaseproof paper, towels, and napkins should be kept well away from the cooking area. On a gas cooker, the ignite button should work, as elderly or disabled people should not be encouraged to use matches.

Heating and cooling hazards

Temperature control in homes for the elderly or disabled, while often overlooked, can be a matter of life or death – in winter and in summer. Central heating is safer than portable heating appliances because elderly and some disabled people are not always able to judge how close they can sit to heat sources. Installing insulation and storm windows will help to maximize heating. Unit or heating controls should be low enough for the user to reach and set. Air conditioning is often too expensive for elderly people, and creating a flow of draughts during a heatwave is extremely important. Window air conditioners should be installed and overhead rotating fan cords should be easy to reach.

STORING GUNS

About half of the total population of the United States keeps a firearm in the home for self-defence purposes. Guns are also sometimes stored in the home or vicinity by those who hunt. It is estimated that, between 1994 and 1998, some 23,776 children under age 19

died from a gun-related injury. These deaths were either accidental or suicide-related. Largely these fatalities occurred as a result of gun owners failing to store their guns effectively. A gun in the home is far more likely to injure a family member than it is ever to be used in a self-defence situation. Despite these facts, an estimated 39 per cent of people in the United States who claim to have guns do not lock them. Many people believe they must keep a loaded gun handy at all times in order to feel secure.

The only way to store a gun safely is to store it unloaded and locked inside a specially designed gun safe or lock box. As even locked cabinets can be pried open, the gun itself should be locked with a special trigger lock. Bullets should be locked away in a separate place. Children and adolescents in the house should either never know the code to the safe or never know the whereabouts of the key, which should be kept well away from household keys. Gun-cleaning supplies should also be locked away, as they are often poisonous to children or pets. Similarly, other potential firearms such as a carpenter's nail gun, BB gun, or an air gun should be locked away and the keys hidden from children's reach.

Lastly, while your gun may be safely locked away, it is important to remember that children can come into contact with guns at neighbour's houses or at school. Teaching them gun safety and instilling in them the importance of avoiding guns altogether is essential.

STOCKPILING FOOD

Stockpiling non-perishable food is a wise precaution against storms, blizzards, or other events that make it difficult to fetch supplies

Gun lock and safe

All guns should be stored in a trigger lock, with the bullets stored in a separate, locked place. Even when trigger locked, guns should always be stowed in locked safes.

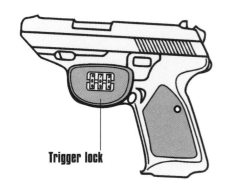

Trigger lock

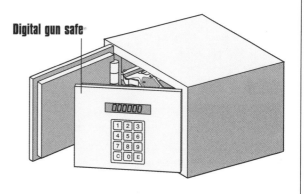

Digital gun safe

or to have them delivered. The best kinds of foods to stockpile are those with a high, concentrated protein and energy yield. Certain foods can be kept in the house at all times, while others can be stockpiled prior to a storm or oncoming blizzard. Making sure that there is a ready supply of bottled water is the most important consideration.

If you have prior warning of a storm or blizzard, you can stock up on extra bottled water, citrus fruits, canned fish, meat, and vegetables, individually packaged juices and drinks that you can take in the car if necessary, raisins and other dried fruits, crackers and dried meats such as salami. You might also stock up on olive oil and condiments such as mustard or sauces that help to liven up servings of rice or canned vegetables.

All food items should be kept in a cool, dark part of the larder, with plenty of ventilation. Food storage areas should be kept scrupulously clean to discourage insect infestations. Grains should be kept in heavy plastic, metal, or glass containers, and any item in a cardboard box should be transferred

to these as larval infestations can penetrate cardboard packaging. Olive oil should be purchased in a metal box to prevent light causing it to oxidize. Stockpiled food should be inspected regularly and sorted for any out-of-date cans, decomposition, or infestation.

Food to stockpile

- Canned fish or meat
- Canned fruits in fruit juice
- Canned cooked beans
- Dried rice, barley, oats
- Dried beans, chickpeas (garbanzos), pulses
- Powdered and/or evaporated milk
- Honey
- Peanut butter
- Fruit juices, vegetable juices
- Stock cubes
- Water purification tablets
- Pet food
- Canned baby food

CHAPTER THREE

Self-defence

Self-defence does not begin with physical confrontation. The first level of self-defence involves avoiding dangerous people and places, and reducing the viability of yourself as a target.

While the next chapter deals with the techniques of physical self-defence, this chapter is arguably the most important. Regardless of your level of self-defence skill, the result of a fight is unpredictable. Many assaults today involve multiple assailants attacking a single individual. In such situations the chances of successfully fighting your way out of the situation are slim. The most effective form of self-defence, therefore, is preventing violence occurring to you in the first place.

In the following chapter, most attackers are described as male. It is an undeniable fact that men account for around 90 per cent of violent incidents outside of the home. They are usually men of between 13 and 17, or 18 and 35 years old, but can include individuals from any race, economic strata, or background.

Female attackers are still rare, though there are worrying trends. In the United States, between 1991 and 1995, convictions of females for violent offences rose from 8045 to 12,400.

In two-thirds of cases, the women had assaulted someone they knew, either a relative or friend. With men, the reverse is true – in most cases, they assault strangers. Of women serving sentences for murder, 53 per cent of their victims were either intimates or relatives, and 21 per cent strangers. Such figures may well change. Many police forces are seeing a worrying rise in female violence, particularly in the context of gangs, and knives and guns are making appearances in female hands. So, although the masculine attacker is assumed in the scenarios of this chapter, an equal awareness of potential female aggressors is essential.

THE THREAT OF VIOLENCE

Violent people are not of uniform type. At one end of the scale is the casual fighter, given to scrapping in bars and other social settings when he feels threatened or slighted. At the other end of the scale is the predatory murderer, someone whose principal aim is to kill his victim. Self-defence begins by closely matching response to threat.

The commonest source of violent threat is from 'incidental' and 'intentional' fighters. An 'incidental' attacker is a person with a tendency to fight in domestic or social situations. The key point is that, although he has a violent personality, he does not pre-plan violence, though he may encourage it to happen and quickly lose self-control.

Aggressors – 'incidental' or 'intentional'?

Incidental fighters are characterized by explosive and excessive reactions. Most of their violence is conducted within social settings, almost always those where alcohol is being consumed. The trigger for the violence can be as little as eye contact with another man. Other causes include arguments over partners, drinks knocked over, or simply the fact that he does not like the look of you. From a self-defence point of view, the problem with the incidental fighter is the frequent lack of logic in his behaviour. His violence may be entirely gratuitous.

Looking for trouble

Little separates the intentional fighter from the incidental fighter. The key distinction is that the intentional fighter has a real affection for assaulting others and may go out looking for trouble. Intentional fighters are often found within the context of crowds, gangs, or groups of men in which the individuals are keen to prove their toughness or attain a higher 'rank' within the group. Intentional fighters usually select victims consciously, generally people whom they perceive as easy targets. Alternatively,

intentional fighters seek out violent encounters with other violent groups – football hooligans are a prime example. Leaders of rival teams of supporters will actually arrange fights at designated times and places. These same gangs have unpredictable tendencies and assault innocents on the slightest pretext.

Street mugging

From attackers who use violence for pleasure or status, we move to attackers who use violence as a means to an end. Many street criminals, for example, assault in order to steal. Note that muggers may rely more on the threat than the reality of violence in order to achieve their goals. Some will simply push the victim against a wall, pull out a knife or other personal weapon, and instruct him to hand over his valuables while threatening violence. Alternatively, he may incapacitate the victim through violence before the theft to make him a compliant target. A key feature of the mugger is that he often uses deception as part of his attack ritual. The actual techniques are studied below, but any means of distracting the victim momentarily before the attack is launched is used.

Violence that can lead to murder

While muggings do occasionally result in deaths, very few violent individuals are committed to killing. Most murders occur spontaneously during arguments or other violent incidents. Killers tend to separate into two camps. First are those who have a particular identifiable victim who is known to them and against whom they have a determined grievance. Secondly, there are killers who select random victims from the general public. A deliberate killing may involve extensive ritual and planning. Victims can well be stalked as a prelude to the violence. They might also receive threatening letters or phone calls. Yet many

Distraction assault

Here the attacker sets up his victim by asking her the time, prior to pulling a knife from a shopping bag. The distraction assault maximizes the shock of the attack, as the victim jumps from a seemingly relaxed situation to one of intense threat. The result is usually shock and compliance on the part of the victim.

murders take place as spur-of-the-moment events, often leading blindly from ferocious arguments. Domestic murders are usually of the latter type. Killers will almost always attack using a weapon, most commonly a knife, gun, or clubbing instrument, or any weapon of opportunity.

THREAT OF RAPE

Rape has many similar patterns of behaviour to killing, but it remains a special category of violence reserved for extended treatment later on in this chapter. The motivations of a rapist can be surprisingly broad. Many rapists convince themselves that their victims actually enjoy the attack and see the intercourse as a way to bolster their self-worth. Some practise it as a more sadistic and predatory activity. The attackers enjoy the sense of power they have over their helpless victims.

Rapes are also committed as revenge attacks – sometimes an ex-boyfriend rapes his former girlfriend as punishment for finishing their relationship. Lastly, there are rapes of simple opportunity against an intoxicated victim too helpless to know what it happening to her body. A key point about rape is that, in most cases, the rapist is known by the victim, often very well. The intimacy that exists in friendship or a relationship can be confused by some men with permissiveness.

KEEPING SAFE ON THE STREET

Security in the home and when travelling on public transport are dealt with in other chapters of this book. What follows are overall guidelines to reduce the likelihood of becoming a victim on the streets.

The first and most obvious point is not to go to places where you increase your personal risk. All urban areas have regions known for high criminal activity, so avoid these at all costs. If you are a stranger to a city, ask a police officer where these areas are located. Get the officer to identify them on a map if possible. Avoid such areas even if travelling by car.

Another sensible precaution is to vary the times and directions you use for routine journeys. If you have regular times and routes for, say, daily shopping, a potential attacker may observe you beforehand and lay an ambush at a future date. Varying routine makes you less predictable and noticeable for any criminal who hangs about in your area. Sometimes,

however, it is unavoidable to change a routine – particularly those revolving around getting to work or taking children to and from school. In this instance, try to find someone with whom you can share the journey. Criminals are far less likely to attack two or more people together. Make sure that your children understand this principle as well.

DANGER ZONES AT NIGHT

When walking around any urban landscape, choose your routes judiciously. Avoid dark or deserted side roads, even if using them shaves time off your journey. Exercise particular caution at night when using streets that have many darkened doorways, entrances to alleyways, poorly lit sections, or large freestanding public waste bins. Such places are ideal for launching a surprise attack. Avoid walking down urban streets that border city parks or waste ground. If you cannot avoid a route, give any potential hiding places as wide a berth as

Drinking and violence

Alcohol is the single greatest external catalyst for acts of violence. Recent studies (see bibliography) have revealed that 87 per cent of murders, 37 per cent of assaults, and 60 per cent of rapes were conducted by offenders under the influence of alcohol. The mechanics of alcohol-related violence are complex. Alcohol impairs judgement, leading an individual to misjudge the reality of a social incident and overreact to it.

Alcohol is also a depressant, so some people become more annoyed and volatile as they drink. This, combined with a reduction in inhibitions, can lead to violence. Normal thinking which might defuse violence is overridden, and the attacker feels a confidence in their physical abilities often mismatched with reality. In addition, men tend to become more sexually aware when they are consuming alcohol (unless heavily intoxicated), raising testosterone levels and aggressive tendencies.

One particular study showed that some groups of people associate the act of drinking alcohol itself with violence. A test group of men given non-alcoholic beers without their knowledge displayed similar levels of violent behaviour as those who were given genuine alcohol. This suggests that, for some men, violence has ingrained itself as a pattern of behaviour that accompanies the social act of drinking. However, it should also be noted that the association of drinking with violence tends only to occur in places where violence is commonplace anyway, indicating a cultural use of aggression.

possible. Swing widely round corners, looking down a street from a distance before venturing along it. Walk as close to the road as possible and always walk facing oncoming traffic.

Some attacks – especially rapes and abductions – are committed from vehicles, so facing the traffic allows you to monitor any suspicious vehicles or drivers. To add a further layer of protection, use streets with a good traffic of people. Attackers generally do not want or like public attention.

STEER CLEAR OF ROWDY CROWDS

The exception to this last rule is if a crowd itself is aggressive, such as you may encounter after a football match or similar sporting event. Keep an eye on the newspapers and media for local sporting events which may attract hostile crowds. Do not venture into city centre public houses and bars on the day of the match, and avoid the immediate area around the sporting ground. When the police are expecting trouble, they tend to construct two separate routes to the sports ground, one for visiting fans and the other for home fans. The visiting fans' route usually leads from the central railway station straight to the sports ground, so it is best to avoid any area between these two landmarks. Try not to use public transport on the day also, particularly subway/tube and mainline trains, for these will be used heavily by the visitors.

Pincer attack

Here one man stops and distracts the woman with a question, while the other circles around the woman's back to make an assault from the rear. A measure to prevent the pincer attack is to walk past the questioner, then turn to put both men in the field of vision.

DON'T TEMPT A THIEF

Taking care with your travel arrangements may be undone if you look like a possible target. First, do not make displays of your wealth which may attract the attention of criminals. Expensive jewellery is a natural magnet for the mugger. Watches, rings, brooches, and neck chains are the most visible. Keep them hidden under clothing or take them off and put them in pockets. When in bars or shops, do not bring out bulging wallets packed with money. If you are carrying a lot of cash, distribute it around your person, and only bring out small amounts at any one time. Take care also when visiting cash machines. Unless there are lots of people around, avoid visiting the ATM at night and especially if there are undesirable characters hanging around.

MAKE BAG-SNATCHING DIFFICULT

Women's handbags are a great temptation for bag-snatchers. When purchasing handbags, try to choose styles that have a long neck strap, as well as a short handgrip. The longer strap should be put over the head and worn across the body; it is an easy matter for a bag to be snatched when held only by the handgrip. For business people carrying briefcases, the same rule applies. Many briefcases or document wallets, however, simply do not have the extended strap fitted, so make sure that you do not carry anything of great value in the case.

CLUBS AND BARS

Bars and nightclubs have always attracted violent individuals. The heavy consumption of alcohol, large groups of men, and sexual competition make for

Concealed knife

A concealed knife positioned ready for a surprise attack. Note that the knife hand has a different configuration from the empty hand, with the fingers curling backwards in a slightly unnatural way.

Warning signals

A mugger makes a classic distraction assault. The warning signal is the single hand in the right pocket. Unless they are carrying something, people tend either to put both

hands in their pockets or to keep them free. A single hand in a pocket is a likely indication that something – possibly a knife or a gun – is being held.

a volatile mix. Often, it is possible to sense the threat of violence building up. Signs of impending violence include: verbal exchanges and pushing; threatening eye contact made across the room; groups of men manoeuvring themselves in relation to other groups; drinks being accidentally spilt; the sound of glass smashing and shouting.

If violence seems a possibility, then simply leave the premises and go somewhere else. Bar fights have the nasty habit of dragging in those around them. If it is difficult to leave the club, or if you are being directly threatened, the best course of action may be to tell the doormen. Describe what is happening and clearly identify the individuals involved. The doormen's response depends upon their profession-alism and training, but most will have a word with the aggressive parties if they think your concern is justified.

In addition, never get involved in verbal domestic disputes unless you 1) truly believe that a vulnerable innocent party is about to be seriously hurt; and 2) feel that you can actually handle the individuals involved if it turns violent. Domestic incidents have an ironic habit of backfiring upon those who intervene. Two individuals may seem full of hatred for one another, but they may both turn upon an outsider if he or she tries to interfere. If you have any concern for how an argument is developing, calling the police should be a first response.

SHOULD YOU GET INVOLVED?

This scenario raises the question of whether you should intervene if someone else is being attacked. The question is impossible to answer neatly. If, for example, you see two men trying forcibly to abduct a child, your personal physical intervention may be the

Concealed screwdriver

Another popular weapon concealment technique is to press the weapon against the thigh. The warning signal is that the weapon arm appears stiff and does not swing like the other arm when the person is walking.

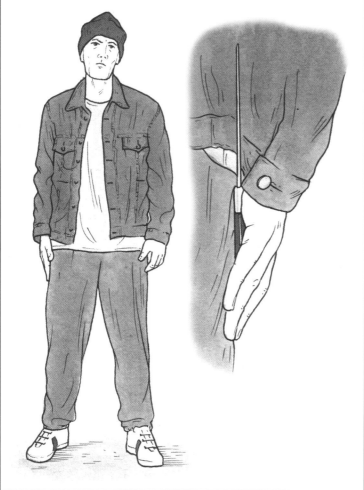

thieves only to be stabbed to death when he actually caught them. As a general rule, try not to become physically involved in violence that you witness. Call the police first. If you have to intervene, shout at the participants from a distance and tell them the police will be here soon. Only do so if you are at a safe distance or within a safe place such as a locked car.

APPEAR CONFIDENT

The final element – perhaps the most important – of violence prevention relates to your general demeanour. Violent people tend to be merciless in the way they chose their victims. Signs of physical or emotional weakness are opportunities in their thinking. They usually want victims who will succumb easily to the assault and offer little threat back to the attacker. If you act weak, agitated, nervous, or vulnerable, you flag yourself up for an attacker.

Regardless of how nervous you feel inside, take charge of your body. Stand up straight using your full height. Tilt your chin slightly upwards and adopt a strong, steady but non-threatening facial expression. When walking do so with an energetic stride and swing of the arms. Attackers are usually nervous of people with good physical fitness, as they generally do not possess it themselves and they could find themselves at physical disadvantage in a fight.

only thing that stops an appalling crime occurring. By contrast, witnessing a woman being held up at knifepoint presents you with a real dilemma. Intervening could easily result in your being stabbed and killed.

A recent event in British newspapers told of a man who chased two common street

SPEAK SLOWLY AND DEEPLY

If you have to communicate with a would-be attacker, do so in a clear and steady voice without trembling. This is easier said than done. Your adrenaline response to the threat constricts the throat and makes breathing shallow, both of which reduce the quality of the voice. To counteract this, take a deep breath through the nose, and speak from your stomach rather than your throat. Tense the diaphragm as you speak – it will support the sound of your voice and give it depth and stability. Also reduce the speed of your speaking voice. Under pressure, speaking pace accelerates, so consciously slowing it will actually produce a normal speaking rhythm. Choose what you say carefully. Speak in short, easily understood sentences, and be clear that you do not want to fight, but will do so if pushed.

By adopting a confident demeanour and taking general precautions against being in the wrong place at the wrong time, most violent threats can be avoided.

HOW TO HANDLE THREATENING BEHAVIOUR

With most physical assaults, there is a period of build-up before blows are actually exchanged. The build-up is the procedure the attacker follows to motivate himself psychologically and physically for the forthcoming violence. Spotting the signs early and knowing how to defuse it will often stop a fight occurring in the first place.

Staring and verbal abuse

Assault build-up usually separates into two types: overt threat and covert threat. The overt threat refers to attacks in which the opponent makes his intentions clear before

Forces that fuel violence

Alcohol and drugs make the biggest contribution to incidents of casual or gratuitous violence, particularly when concentrated in a drinking environment such as a bar or nightclub.

● MALE–FEMALE DYNAMICS
Competition between men for the attention of women in public places is a danger area. When reinforced by drink, men often mix sexual predation with a heightened awareness of competitors, and so can use violence as a way of displacing unrequited sexual emotions and 'removing' the competition.

● VERBAL AGGRESSION
Many fights begin with a verbal argument or exchange of abuse. The exchange may turn to violence if 1) one party begins to lose the argument and feels that violence is his only recourse; 2) the argument raises physical gesturing to an extreme, making fighting a natural progression; and 3) one party feels socially belittled by the exchange and attacks to resolve the conflict.

● EYE CONTACT
In a behavioural context, prolonged eye contact between strangers, and

especially between men, is often interpreted as a threat. The staring is an attempt psychologically to defeat the opponent and force him to back down. Many fights begin with little more than locked eyes, again especially if the participants have been drinking.

● POVERTY
Clearly, poverty increases theft-related violence and drink-related violence. The levels of violence tend to be worse within the economically disadvantaged community itself, rather than encroaching on more affluent areas.

actual violence occurs. It usually begins with bold, direct eye contact. An attacker may well close distance with you and stare into your eyes from close range as a method of psychological intimidation. The close-range stare is usually accompanied by a series of provocative and threatening verbal assault. Usually this assault involves short questions mixed heavily with expletives. 'What are you ******* looking at?' and 'Have you got a ******* problem?' are common examples.

Squaring up for a fight

The verbal assault is often accompanied by aggressive finger jabbing and head thrusting to emphasise each point. The attacker will usually splay his arms out to the sides as he approaches you to make himself appear physically large. The questioning may turn into a challenge or direct threat the closer the individual approaches violence, such as 'I'm gonna smash your face in'. Usually by this point the fists begin to rise into a fight position. This can be a useful moment. If the attacker angles his body away from you and adopts a professional-looking guard, it may indicate a good fighter. If, however, the opponent remains squarely facing you – a position exposing all his main body targets for attack – he could well be an immature fighter or simply overconfident. Either way, the body posture will dictate your physical response should the encounter come to blows.

The sentences the attacker uses usually become shorter and shorter as he leads up to the actual assault. The final signals may be compact single words such as 'Yeah' or 'C'mon', repeated frequently as he tries to work up an explosive breathing pattern for the attack. Note that in this scenario that if the attacker is particularly nervous he may not speak at all because fear has constricted his throat and breathing. In this case, listen to the attacker's breathing patterns. Breathing usually becomes faster and louder just prior to an assault.

How to avert an attack

The procedure for dealing with this threat is to tackle it as early as possible. At the eye-contact stage, try not to meet the stare and simply back down and go elsewhere. If the attacker is at close range, however, and is making a verbal assault, this is rarely possible. You have two elements available to your response: 1) psychological dissuasion; and 2) physical dissuasion.

Talk your way out of trouble

Psychological dissuasion means either reducing the opponent's aggression levels or intimidating him enough to back off. The first option is the best option. If you can make the assailant laugh, reason with him, or aggrandize him in front of his friends, then he may well back down. Say clearly that you do not want to fight and that you will go elsewhere if need be. One other advantage of this approach is that the assailant's levels of adrenaline will dip, and he may lower his mental guard, opening the way for you to make a surprise pre-emptive attack if you feel it necessary. Be careful about appearing too weak and defeated, however. It is unlikely to win you pity from the aggressor and may only serve to spur on his violence, as he sees you as a soft target.

Act crazy

In many instances, however, the nice approach simply does not work. The intimidatory approach has more emotional risk, but can pay dividends. Your goal is make the opponent believe you will be a tough customer should he opt for violence. This strategy demands some role-playing on your part, although the high levels of adrenaline coursing through your body will help to give you credibility.

Adopt a demeanour which conveys a willingness to fight. There are several options. First, pretend that you are bordering on the psychopathic. Summon up all your

Signs of potential violence

The aggressor makes beckoning motions to his opponent, either using his fingers or both hands, and usually reinforced with single-syllable threats.

The head is thrust violently forwards to emphasise shouted threats and verbal abuse.

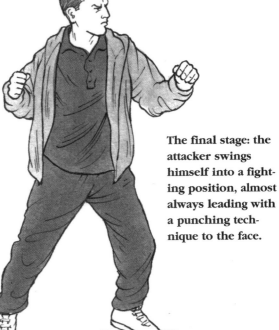

The final stage: the attacker swings himself into a fighting position, almost always leading with a punching technique to the face.

Prior to an attack, the aggressor (unless well trained) will usually squeeze his face into a tight expression, dropping the eyebrows downwards and clenching the jaw.

fear and adrenaline, and channel it into ferocious verbal threats, a wild and agitated appearance, and strange behaviour such as twitching. Dribbling saliva, staring wildly, and shouting out nonsense phrases will all serve to reinforce the picture. Your intention is to alarm the assailant into thinking that you are about to go berserk, hopefully leading him to back down from you through fear of violent confrontation.

Prepare to defend yourself

A similar but less outlandish approach may be simply to meet fire with fire. Return his stare and threats equally. If the assailant invites you to fight, verbally accept the offer with confidence and menace. The ideal result is that the assailant backs down and goes away. Obviously, you must be prepared for the attacker meeting you every step of the way and moving towards physical

Establishing a protective space

Raising the hands outwards in a guard position serves three functions: it creates a psychological barrier for the assailant to cross, it gives the defender a protective zone around him or herself, and it allows a quick move into attacking techniques. Note how unthreatening the guard can appear.

violence. The confidence to threaten your potential assailant usually only comes after some substantial self-defence training. You must be prepared to fight the fight as well as talk the fight.

Stand your ground

The physical response to intimidation needs to be as strong as the verbal response. A key element is to adopt a protective guard. If you are right-handed, step forwards with the left leg and angle the body at 45 degrees to your opponent. Raise your open hands – not closed fists, which are an overt invitation to fight – and hold them up in front of you, the left in front of the right. Use the hands to establish a protective zone around you. If the assailant is pushing forwards, use the front hand to restrain him gently. The open hands will appear unthreatening, and you can make demonstrative hand gestures to back up any verbal pleading or threatening. Crucially, as the opponent touches your hands you gain information about distancing should you have to resort to punches or kicks. The guard will also alert the attacker that you are no physical pushover.

If the attacker is becoming particularly aggressive, use the front hand of the guard to deliver a hard shove to the chest which sends him sprawling backwards. Once he is out of ranges yell a loud and explosive verbal warning, such as 'Stay there!'. The combination of the push and the shout sometimes results in a rush of adrenaline throughout the opponent's body which he interprets as fear. This technique may suffice to prompt him to stay away.

The guard is useful for a number of reasons, not least because it can tell you when violence is about to begin. If an assailant barges into your guard several times, and uses the threatening gestures noted above, he is likely to follow through on his attack. If you cannot defuse the situation, strike first.

Scan for danger

One final caution. As you are remonstrating with a potential attacker, look out for any friends of his closing in around you, taking advantage of your distraction. Some of the most dangerous attacks begin by deception.

COVERT THREATS

Mugging someone and killing someone are very different crimes, but they frequently have similar build-up routines. The key ingredient is deception. Deception is used to lower the victim's guard or distract him from a potential threat and strike in the moment of lowered awareness.

The deception tactic alters according to whether the attack is made by one individual or more. A single individual will tend to approach as if on some other matter. Asking the time or for directions are common methods of distraction. What the attacker is looking for is the moment you relax your guard and take your eyes off him. In addition, the apparently innocent purpose of the approach allows the attacker to close distance with you. Once you are distracted, a concealed knife is drawn, you are pushed against a wall or other surface, then robbed or worse.

Suspicious behaviour

Detecting and avoiding the covert assault involves a more subtle awareness of signs than for the overt attacker. Look at the general appearance of the individual. Many muggers today almost wear a kind of uniform consisting of a hooded jacket with the hood pulled over a baseball cap. The hood and cap shield their faces and hair, and so limit the amount of identifying characteristics on display. This is their precaution against identification should they be caught.

If you can see their face clearly, more clues of their intentions are available. They may be continually looking from side to side – they are checking constantly for anyone else around. Their complexion may

Confident posture

Standing straight, pulling the shoulders back, and adopting a confident expression all reduce your chances of being selected for a violent assault – and signal someone who will defend.

be pale with nerves, and they will generally be unsmiling unless they are very practised in deception. They may be nervously toying with part of their clothing. They might also shiver with nerves. A more worrying external sign is indication that they are concealing a knife. A hand pressed close to the side of the body suggests that they are hiding something, as does a single hand kept inside a coat pocket when talking (most people reveal their hands when meeting someone for the first time).

Check all around you

The covert attacker may be working in tandem with someone else, holding your attention while someone approaches from the rear. The aim is that one person will surprise you and hold you, while the other commits the robbery or similar violent act. Watch out for individuals approaching in pairs or groups at a distance, but then splitting up when approaching you. Use your peripheral vision to monitor everyone's movement, and position yourself so that no one can approach from a blind side.

Take the lead

If approached by anyone of whom you are suspicious, try to manoeuvre away from them by crossing the road, entering a shop, and so on. If there is no way of avoiding him and he is heading straight up to you, stop him at a distance with a gentle verbal warning such as 'Could you stop there, please?' Raise your hands into a guard position as protection and to show you are serious. If you have made a mistake about the person, you can simply apologise and explain your thinking, which is better than allowing yourself to be mugged or otherwise assaulted. Direct your eyesight to the centre of his chest. This focus allows you to monitor all limb movements equally and so make an early detection of a knife.

If the person ignores your demand and continues his advance, be prepared to fight.

Start shouting and screaming for help. Shove the person backwards hard, and issue a warning. In most cases, the measures described so far will be enough to stop a continuation of the attack. The covert attacker is looking for an easy opening to the assault, and the opportunity has gone. If the attacker simply comes back, then you should have recourse to the self-defence techniques outlined in the next chapter.

RAPE

The violence used in rape attacks varies wildly in degree. Sometimes a rapist will rely on the paralysing fear of the victim to commit his crime unopposed, after which he leaves. Some rapists have even been known to try to arrange a date with the victim after the attack, such is their warped vision of intimacy.

Distancing

If being threatened, maintain a non-fighting distance if at all possible. This allows the **potential attacker the room to back down and de-escalate the situation.**

Other rapists, however, are intent on murder. Killing is either a part of their fantasy or an attempt to get rid of the primary witness.

Rape attacks fall into three basic categories. The highest percentage of rapes are committed by people known to the victim – boyfriends, friends, even relatives. Rapes by these people involve complex patterns of interaction beforehand and sometimes even consensual sexual behaviour. They are nonetheless dangerous for this, and the rapist is just as likely to use serious forms of violence during his attack as other types of rapist.

A different type of rapist is unknown to the victim, but practises deceit to gain their confidence and manoeuvre them into place for an attack. They may lull their victim into lowering their guard using a very convincing 'nice guy' act. It is not uncommon for rape victims to recount their shock at how an apparently normal and charming man could turn into such a monster. It is sad to say, but you must mistrust anyone's motives until you truly know them.

Lastly, there are rapists who ambush the victim without any attempt at social interaction beforehand. They tend to launch the ambush in places where the rape can take place unhindered by passers-by, such as parks, large gardens, or stretches of waste-land. A van or car may also be used to abduct

Threat avoidance

This street is ideal for attackers: the steps restrict a victim's movement, while the **doorway and overhanging trees provide features to conceal an ambush.**

HOW TO AVOID SEXUAL ATTACK

If the person is known to you, beware of constant minor sexual advances, even if they seem harmless. If you do not want the advances, say so, but if they persist or intensify put some time and distance between you and the other person. Avoid spending time alone with the person. Meet him in a public place, and do not travel home with him alone in his car. Tell a friend about your concerns, and try to make sure he or she is present if the person calls around at your home.

Be clear about acceptable behaviour

If you go home with a man for coffee after a date, be clear that coffee is all that is on the menu (movies unhelp-fully depict the invitation for coffee as an invitation for sex, and many men still interpret it as this). The most important rule is that you make yourself plain about what is acceptable and what is not. Potential rapists often have highly developed fantasy lives. They will interpret many signals of friendship as

the victim, particularly if there is more than one person participating in the rape.

Whatever its degree or result, rape is an appalling crime with serious physical and emotional results. Preventing such an attack is not always feasible – it is impossible to live in a state of hypervigilance about every man you come across. Yet there are precautions.

sexual flirtation, so must be dissuaded in no uncertain terms. Should a person go ahead in his advances, tell him very firmly that what he is attempting will constitute rape or sexual assault. The seriousness of the terminology and possible consequences may serve to snap the potential rapist out of his fantasy and awaken him to what he is doing.

If you are in a relationship with the other person, be as firm about establishing sexual boundaries. Many rapes occur as developments from heavy petting. Let the person know exactly what you do not want to happen, and stop any attempts to go beyond your limits as soon as possible.

Remain aware of how much you are drinking. Alcohol can warp your judgement about a person while increasing flirtation. In addition, men frequently become sexually adventurous when drunk and are less likely to respond to subtle hints that they are not going to get their way.

'Date rape' drugs

Be very careful who buys you drinks. Many of the so-called 'date-rape' incidents have involved the drug Rohypnol, a powerful sedative used properly to combat sleeping disorders and also as a pre-anaesthetic. In rape incidents, the drug is usually slipped into the victim's drink, the rape taking place some hours later. Do not let people who you do not know buy you drinks, especially if you are on your own. Also, have a friend guard your glass while you are in the restroom, or, if you are on your own, down the drink before going out.

If a person is making unwanted sexual advances is in your home and they refuse to leave, call the police, preferably using a phone out of earshot. If this is not possible, leave your house and go to a neighbour's home. Ask them to call the police, and wait there until they arrive.

Car parks

Inner-city car parks are common places for assaults. The parked vehicles allow attackers to hide and prepare ambushes. Proximity to housing and streets means the attacker can make convenient escape after the attack. Lighting in the car park itself is poor, making it shadowy and dangerous at night.

Dealing with a stalker

- First of all, call the police.
- Stalkers see any response from you as a reward for the stalking. Therefore give an initial 'no' to his or her advances, then never respond personally to them again.
- Change your routes to work or the shops.
- Change the times of your routines.
- Record any phone calls from the stalker on an answering machine. Keep the tapes for police evidence. Do not change your main phone number, but use this to record the messages. Use a private cell phone or another line for all other calls. Tell friends and family to call you only on this number.
- Keep a log of all the stalker's activity. Include as much information as possible.
- Take a self-defence class.
- Request that your address be removed from publicly held records such as electoral registers.
- Contact local stalking support groups. They will be able to give you professional advice and much reassurance.

Predatory rapists who select unknown victims use entirely different tactics. They usually attempt some deceit as a prelude to attack. Follow the principles above for dealing with muggers. Do not let anyone unfamiliar approach too closely, and control the distance with your voice and posture. Rapists tend to stalk victims beforehand. Warning signs are:

- Someone who watches you closely, but whose gaze snatches away when you look at them.
- Someone who shadows your movements from a distance. Watch particularly if a person walks past you, but then reverses direction to follow you.
- Monitor a person's hands. If one or both are never removed from a pocket, it could indicate a concealed weapon.

Look tough to deter the rapist

If someone appears to be watching or following you, make it clear that you are on to him. Return a hard, defiant stare or firmly tell him to back off. Do not, however, tackle the person at close range, and make sure that

Rohypnol

Rohypnol is the popular name for flunitrazepam. Made in Europe and Latin America (it is illegal in the United States), Rohypnol is used to treat insomnia and also as a pre-anaesthetic. It is an extremely powerful drug, with a sedative effect 10 times that of Valium.

Rohypnol has become commonly used by drug addicts in conjunction with other narcotics such as cocaine and heroin. However, it has also been used to incapacitate victims prior to raping them. The drug has no taste or smell, so can be ingested unwittingly in a drink.

Ingesting Rohypnol brings effects within 10 minutes. The victim becomes mentally confused and suffers from poor body control. She may feel hot and cold at the same time and experience nausea. Judgement and self-control also deteriorate. If combined with alcohol, Rohypnol can produce periods of blackout known to last between 8 and 24 hours. It is usually in this period that the rape occurs.

After recovery, the victim often has no recollection whatsoever of what happened to them over the preceding period.

Information source: The National Women's Health Information Center, US Dept. of Health and Human Services

Social threats

Nightclubs and bars are among the commonest locations for violent assault. Be particularly aware of situations – as pictured here – where men significantly outnumber women, and consumption of drink is high. Position yourself away from noisy or aggressive groups of men, and avoid eye contact with any of them.

you remain in places where there are lots of people. Rape is no different from other forms of violence in that the attacker prefers a compliant victim. Someone looking switched on with a tough attitude does not fit this profile, and the rapist is likely to lose interest and switch his attentions elsewhere.

Shout, punch, kick, and scream

This final point is essential should you actually be the victim of an attempted rape. Self-defence expert Geoff Thompson points out that all statistics show that women who fight back furiously against a rapist have a greater chance of avoiding the actual rape and of staying alive. Unfortunately, rape victims are often so rigid with fear that they simply comply with the rapist's desires.

A woman who struggles, bites, kicks, punches, and scratches brings personal risk to the rapist, and he is likely to break off the attack. Remember that rapists will have little pity or mercy. Their assurances of 'Do what I want and you won't get hurt' count for nothing. If the rape is evidently highly planned and takes place over a long period of time, the attack may well end in murder as the rapist attempts to cover his tracks and get rid of the primary witness. Better to resist with all strength than go down the rapist's dark road. Fighting back with physical means is the subject of our next chapter.

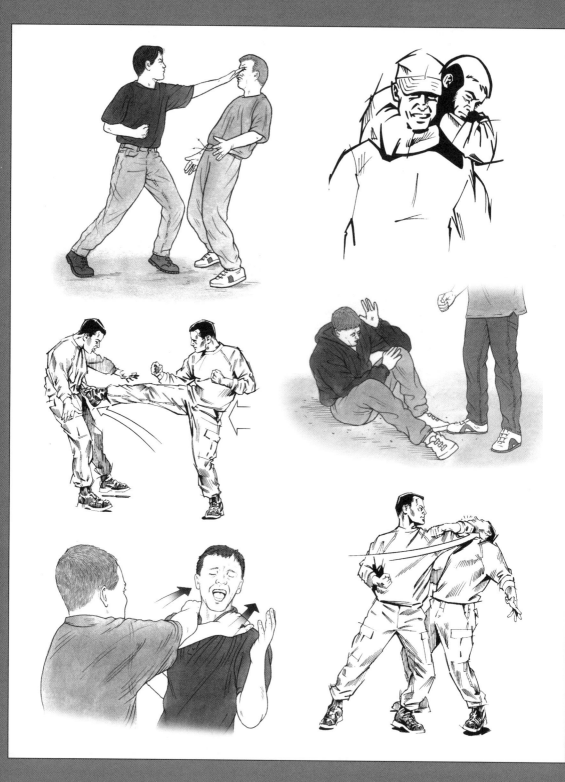

CHAPTER FOUR

Safety on the streets

Many unarmed combat techniques formally taught are totally inadequate for the task of self-preservation in real life situations. Simple but effectives methods are called for in the streets.

While complex wristlocks, precision strikes, and advanced take-down moves may work fluidly in a training hall under controlled and manageable conditions, the reality of street fighting is quite different and requires more elementary techniques.

BRUTE FORCE DEFEATS SKILL

Tests under training conditions showed that even experienced martial artists had almost no opportunity to apply sophisticated techniques in non-choreographed and ruleless circumstances. In fact, they were able to use less than 10 per cent of their self-defence repertoire. Most ended up submitting to less experienced but violently intent opponents, for several reasons.

First, their opponent was utterly determined and used all their physical and psychological means to inflict defeat. Secondly, the defenders were almost paralysed with an adrenaline rush of fear they had never experienced before. Lastly, they were unable to inflict decisive punishment on the constantly moving and attacking opponent. The training situations simply did not reflect reality. Fighting is a crude and brutal practice, and anything which purports to make it clinical or easy is misguided.

SELF-DEFENCE REALISM

Realism is a top priority in unarmed-combat training. Its importance hinges on the brain's response to unfamiliar or traumatic situations.

Imagine the brain as an infinitely complex filing cabinet. Each experience we have receives its own 'file' composed of all sensory, physical, and emotional data relating to the event. When we encounter a repeat of the experience, the file is reused to find the correct response. The file is also expanded with additional information, including comparisons with other relevant files.

Experience files take time to construct. When we learn to drive, for example, each manipulation of the gears and clutch is a deliberate, difficult, and conscious process. When we have actually learnt to drive – when the file is full of 'gear-changing' information – then the process becomes automatic. Should we encounter novel situations, the brain will pull out the most relevant file and use it to interpret and act, and also build up a new file.

Developing a 'fight file'

Unarmed combat training needs to produce a 'fight file'. This file should elicit an automatic defence response when attacked or threatened. Those who do not have it are often undone by surges of adrenaline, fear, anxiety, and confusion – their brains are lacking any reference for correct response. Unarmed combat training must contain the following practices to provide a dependable mental model:

- Wear normal street clothing during some training sessions. Clothing limits body movement (heavy boots, for example, retard kicks), so it is better to discover and adjust to these limitations in the training environment.

- Aim for realism: once techniques are learnt, practise them within aggressive and realistic role-playing scenarios. Props such as chairs and tables can be placed in the training area to hinder movement. Other students can act as a crowd to provide a claustrophobic nightclub feel. Foul language, violent threats, and insults, almost always part of a fight encounter, should be used without restraint (though only within the specific combat scenario). Demeanour must be aggressive and purposeful. Outside of these exercises, students should always be disciplined and controlled.

- Step outside the comfort zone: place yourself under real pressure. 'Real

Fight patterns

Detailed academic studies of actual fights reveal a distinct pattern to violent encounters.

- There is a short verbal exchange of threats and abuse while the two participants close distance.
- A flurry of punches and strikes are directed at the head and body, usually at very close ranges of

46–60cm (18–24in). The punches often end the fight with either a knockout or incapacitating injury.

- If these punches do not end the fight, it then descends into a grappling contest, during which time the participants usually fall to the ground. There the fight is decided through a varied range of crude chokes,

scratching, and gouging techniques.

- If one of the participants is backed by a group of friends, they will often start kicking his opponent while he is on the ground, frequently to the point of unconsciousness.
- Crucially, the whole process usually takes little more than 4 seconds.

pressure' means the genuine possibility of being hurt in training. Only when this possibility is present will the student accustom himself or herself to adrenaline responses and fear, and the body shakes that accompany both. Something has to be at stake or otherwise the student will settle into a mental comfort zone.

- Make no concessions: pair up with training partners of any size or gender. Larger opponents must not restrain their techniques against smaller partners. It does not help a student to give them a leeway they would not experience in a real fight. In addition, proper self-defence techniques should work on anyone, regardless of size.

- 'Freestyle' sparring sessions should be part of the regular training regime. Within these, any techniques can be used and the only rules present should be those to prevent particularly serious injury (for example, no eye-gouging, strangulation, or kicks to the head – a proper submission procedure is required). The benefits of these types of session are an increased understanding of the unpredictability of fighting, as well as an ability to keep thinking under the

Defensive body posture

The man on the left has correct defensive body posture, angling his torso and abdomen away from his **opponent and so reducing target opportunities. The man on the right unwittingly exposes all his target areas.**

extreme stress of combat. Only conduct freestyle sparring, however, under the guidance of a sensible referee.

Eye strike

A seemingly innocuous defensive position can be switched in an instant into a jab or an eye strike (seen here). Note how the man on the right has been taken completely by surprise, and how the man on the left is pushing off his back leg to drive body weight into the strike. His right hand is preparing to deliver a second blow, in case the first is indecisive.

When training pays off

Martial arts clubs often avoid such tough training parameters because of the intimidating atmosphere they create (also because of insurance arrangements). In fact, this is exactly the right type of atmosphere for teaching self-defence skills, as long as it is not gratuitous or unintelligent. The pressure of training will harden the responses to fighting and allow training to take over in the case of a real attack.

VULNERABLE POINTS

All self-defence techniques need to be directed against vulnerable parts of the human body to have decisive results. Many martial arts commonly list around 30 body targets. Such lengthy lists of vulnerable points are, in street fighting, mostly impractical. An accessible body target is one open to assault when the opponent is moving vigorously, not standing pliantly in front of his opponent passively offering his body for target selection, as happens in many training scenarios.

Applying this criterion significantly reduces the number of available body targets to around seven or eight, but these are the genuine fight winners.

Head targets

The human head offers the densest cluster of accessible body targets. The skull itself provides few opportunities (unless armed with a club or similar weapon). It is immensely strong and more likely to cause broken bones if struck with a fist.

Go for the eyes

Eyes, alternatively, are extremely vulnerable. Gouging or poking techniques can result in scratched, collapsed, or even displaced (removed from the eye sockets) eyeballs. All are serious injuries, possibly leading to permanent blindness. The problem is that the eyes are well-protected by a reflex action – the eyelids close and the head snatches

backwards the instant an eye attack is perceived. Consequently, eye attacks need to be either very fast or a gouging action to achieve results.

Strike the nose

The nose is the next prominent face target. When struck hard, the nose bleeds, breaks, or produces watering eyes which temporarily blind the opponent. Theoretically, a hard nose strike can kill by driving the nasal bone up into the brain cavity, but this is very unlikely. Even a broken nose is rarely a fight stopper, so the value of a nose attack lies mainly in distracting the opponent or producing a time gap for delivering another technique.

Grab and bite the ears

Ears are accessible, but in a fight results are mixed. The most commonly taught ear attack is the cup strike. Both ears are struck simultaneously with cupped hands. Air compression theoretically results in ruptured eardrums. Applying the technique on a struggling opponent, however, is difficult. Far better to attack the ears by gripping and tearing them or, as unpalatable as it sounds, biting them. The nose is also vulnerable to a bite, and the pain of such an attack is absolutely excruciating.

A firm blow to the jaw

The jaw is the possibly best of all head targets. It is lined with sensitive nerve endings. If struck in the right spot and hard enough, the opponent will be knocked unconscious through a shaken brain effect (the brain strikes against the inside of the skull wall as the head is spun). Even if knockout does not occur, the jaw may fracture or dislocate, both fight-stopping injuries. Jaw attacks require solid and accurate punching technique to achieve results.

A danger of a jaw knockout is that the unconscious individual's head can drop

Cross punch

The cross punch utilizes the power of the hips to generate a potentially knockout blow.
As the right fist makes contact, the puncher swings his right hip violently forwards behind the technique, thus delivering his full body weight behind the punch. By hitting the jaw the puncher is most likely to inflict a fight-stopping injury.

unrestrained onto the pavement or similar hard surface. Fatalities can and do occur from such a drop.

Chest targets

The solar plexus is the soft point in the centre of the chest just beneath the breast-bone. It has no muscular covering (although pectoral and abdominal muscles act as 'sentries'), and a hard strike to this point usually 'winds' the opponent. More serious injury and even death occurs if the stomach, liver, or gall bladder is torn or ruptured.

Vulnerable ribs

Another chest target is the floating ribs, the lowest pair of ribs. Floating ribs are not con-nected to the breastbone. They are easily bent inwards and broken by a kick or punch. Any rib may fracture under a hard blow. A punctured lung may result if the sharp end of the fractured bone penetrates the lung sac.

In practice, however, the chest is a tricky fight target. A solar plexus is hard to locate on a moving individual, and even broken ribs may go unnoticed by an adrenaline- or drink-fuelled individual. Use these targets only for 'softening' or distracting the opponent if no other targets are available. Torso targets in general are best restricted to finishing stamps or kicks while the opponent is on the ground.

Joint targets

These are plentiful around the human skeleton. In self-defence, joints are either broken by pulling them back beyond their natural range of movement or locked at the extremity of their movement to control a limb. The major joints in the arms and legs are extremely difficult to control during a fluid combat situation. Powerful muscles in the limbs make guiding the joint into a locking or breaking position problematic, although there are one or two suitable techniques you can employ.

Knee joints can be damaged by kicking, although considerable kicking accuracy and speed are required to do so.

Some of the best joints to attack are those in the fingers. If the opportunity presents

The last resort

The throat is the target area of last resort. Striking the throat can easily result in a fatality: the windpipe collapses, causing suffocation; blood flow to the brain is stopped through damaging the jugular vein; the vagus or laryngeal nerves either side of the windpipe suffer contusions and cause heart stoppage; even the spinal column can be fatally damaged.

Such terrible consequences should not stop you learning throat attacks. At punching distance, the throat is best assaulted using a jab punch, a chopping motion with the side of the hand, or by jabbing stiffened fingers directly into the windpipe. At close range, the larynx can be gripped between thumb and fingers and compressed, causing pain, unconsciousness or even death if the windpipe is crushed. A choking grip using the forearm, inner elbow joint, or hands is another option.

A medical point to consider is that, if only the windpipe is compressed, unconsciousness takes up to and over 30 seconds to set in. If the pressure is maintained after unconsciousness, death would result in less than 2 minutes. However, if the jugular veins either side of the windpipe are pressed in hard, the blood flow to the brain is severed, unconsciousness arrives in around 4 seconds, and death in as little as 30 seconds.

itself, fingers can be gripped and snapped backwards; they break easily. A broken finger or thumb often prevents the attacker using the hand for further gripping or punching.

Groin targets

The testicles are usually classified as a fail-safe fight-winning target. Certainly a knee, foot, or fist connecting squarely with the testicles will induce a powerful nausea and sickening pain in the victim, sometimes even unconsciousness. Yet surprisingly, testicle strikes win few fights. A reflex flinch reaction pulls the testicles in between the thighs when an attack is spotted, and there they are well protected against all but the most powerful blows. Grabbing and squeezing the testicles offers greater chances of success, although thick trousers and underwear are surprisingly protective against even a strong grip.

The arguments against a testicle shot should be discarded if the target is clearly presented, as the effects of a clean strike will usually end the fight. Yet the abdominal area in general is severely vulnerable to attack in both males and females. The groin contains the bladder and several vital arteries and veins. A heavy impact into the area will certainly produce pain. Circulatory shock and internal bleeding, and even death through clotting in the femoral vein, are more serious consequences.

The list of body targets above is not exhaustive. The kidney area either side of the lower back is vulnerable to painful hook punches and strikes. A heavy blow to the nape of the neck can damage or even break the spinal column. Feet are exposed to crushing by stamping kicks, and shins can produce debilitating pain if kicked with heavy boots. The targets above are selected because they are accessible and have the right qualities to influence a fight in your favour. Furthermore, knowing too many body targets may result in fatal indecision during combat. The basic principle: choose an open body target and attack it hard. Your aim, remember, is to stop the opponent from being able to fight, not just hurting him.

HOW TO MAKE A FIST

Punching properly is undoubtedly your greatest self-defence asset. Above anything else, good punching and striking skills will decide a fight.

First, you must make a correct fist. A poorly structured fist often ends up broken in a fight. To make a correct fist, curl the fingers tightly into the palm of the hand. Place the joint of the thumb on the outside of the index finger between the first and second joints. Next, squeeze the fingers together using pressure between the thumb and the little finger. If you turn your hand palm up, you will notice an arched pattern made by the finger joints. The structure is often described in architectural terms as an arched bridge. The middle finger is in effect the keystone, and the thumb and little fingers provide the foundation stones to make the whole structure secure.

The striking point when punching is the two largest knuckles. To protect the bones of the hand on impact, the back of the hand should be level with the top of forearm and the two largest knuckles working in a straight line with the forearm bones.

Types of punch

There are four main types of punch: jab, cross, uppercut, and hook. Each will be examined in turn, but there are some general points about delivery. When punching, keep the arm as relaxed as possible during its flight to the target. Relaxed, soft muscle expands and contracts with greater speed than tense muscle. Maintaining a loose arm results in a faster punch. Only at the point of impact is it essential to tense the arm and all major muscle groups in the body from the feet to the shoulders.

Screw punch

'Screwing' a punch into the target dramatically increases its effect and penetration. The punching fist is kept palm up throughout most of its flight until it just makes contact with the target. Then it is screwed into the target until the palm faces downwards. Retracting the opposite fist in a contrary motion adds to the power of the punch through body torsion.

Put your weight behind a punch

The sudden tension at the end of the technique channels more of the body weight into the punch. Body-weight transference is paramount to self-defence. A 63kg (140lb) man may be at a fighting disadvantage against a 100kg (224lb) man, but if he punches (or kicks for that matter) with 63kg (140lb) of force, he will have no trouble knocking out his opponent. The general principle is that the body mass must be pushed behind the punch using the legs, and the shoulder and hip of the punching-arm side driven forwards hard on impact. In addition, the front foot can be lifted slightly off the floor as the punch strikes, so that the full body weight is taken on the fist.

The following techniques are described as if in the left-side forward extended guard: left leg forwards, body angled at 45 degrees, chin tucked down, hands framing the face in a guard, and elbows tucked into the chest to protect the ribs. If you are left-handed and prefer to lead with your right foot, then reverse the following instructions.

The jab

The jab – delivered with the front hand – is invaluable for its speed and stunning effect. From the guard position, the left fist is thrust in a straight line into the target. On impact, the palm of the hand twists downwards to face the floor, screwing the punch deep into the target and increasing its force. Pull the left shoulder almost up to the cheek and look along the arm to improve accuracy. Drive the left side of the body sharply forwards to apply the body weight. Keep the right hand in its original position to guard against a counterattack.

The cross

Probably the most powerful punch of all, the cross is delivered with the rear hand, in this case the right. The fist is fired at the target, but at the moment of impact the right hip and the right shoulder are pushed violently forwards. Further body-weight transference is achieved by pushing the entire body into the punch using the right foot. The cross is the true knockout punch, but requires considerable practice to ensure all its elements coordinate and lock on impact. Once they do, it is a decisive self-defence tool.

The hook

The hook is thrown from either side and is a classic boxer's punch for close-range encounters. If using the right hand, the fist is thrown in a semicircular motion with the target usually the side of the opponent's head or jaw. The right hip is pushed forwards and round to follow the arc of the punch. An important point is to keep the palm of the punching hand facing towards you. If the palm is facing downwards, there is the danger that the joints of the little finger and ring finger will take the impact and be broken. Lifting the front foot and shifting the body to the left will give the punch full body weight. The hook performed with the front hand is rarely as powerful, but the technique remains the same.

The uppercut

The uppercut punch is a similar to the hook, but rises vertically upwards to connect beneath the opponent's chin, rather than swing in from the side. In the case of a right hook, the fist is fired in an upward-rising vertical line. On impact, the feet raise up the entire body, and the right hip is pushed upwards. Like the hook, the palm of the punching fist is kept facing towards the puncher. Squatting the body down as a prelude to the punch increases the upward force of delivery, as the legs have room for a more significant upward thrust. Both the hook and the uppercut are difficult punches to spot coming in, as they operate at the peripheries of the opponent's vision. This explains why they account for most boxing knockouts.

Elbow strikes

Elbow strikes generate enormous power at close ranges. Here the elbow is driven sideways across the front of the chest into the opponent's chin. At the moment of impact, the attacker expands his chest forcefully outwards and pushes sideways with his right leg to increase the impact. This jab may result in a knockout or a broken jaw.

Training equipment

When training punches and kicks, three pieces of equipment are useful – a punchbag, strike shield, and focus mitts. A punchbag is essentially a heavy cloth-filled sack suspended from the ceiling or on a wall bracket. It provides substantial weight resistance and demands powerful techniques to move it significantly. The strike shield is a large, rectangular pad filled with impact foam. It is held by a training partner who grips it close to their body. Hitting the pad does not hurt the holder, but the level at which their stability is affected by the blow gives you a good indication of what effect the techniques would have on a real person.

Lastly, focus mitts are two small circular pads worn by the training partner as gloves. They are used to build up punching speed and accuracy. An excellent training method is for the partner to present the focus mitts briefly as targets, alternating their position each time. Your role is to strike them hard in the one or two seconds they are visible, training fast responses and quick punch selection.

HARD WORK, BUT HIGH REWARDS

Once you have mastered the individual punching techniques, practise using them in combinations. Keep up a steady flow of techniques against the punchbag or other target, alternating the type of punch constantly, but maintaining the power and speed. Adjust footwork constantly to give you the right distancing. Maintaining the flow of punches is exhausting if you have not experienced it before. Self-defence must be conducted in tandem with a programme of fitness training. Even against a streetwise fighter you will probably win if his fitness levels are poor and you can take him beyond the first 20–30 seconds of combat.

Punch into and through

To allow your punching talents to work in an actual fight, obey several rules. Distancing is crucial. The aim is to punch into and through the target. If, for instance, the target is the tip of the jaw, the end point of the punch is effectively the back of the head. Also follow the 'hit and stick' principle. Allow the punch to remain 'stuck' to the target for a fraction of a second (do not leave it there too long or the arm will be grabbed). This allows all the energy of the strike to transfer into the target.

Never signal a punch

In all attacking techniques, do not 'telegraph' your movements. When untrained people fight, they tend to make unconscious movements prior to attacking (some of these are discussed in the previous chapter). Being aware of these movements gives enormous advantage, as you can read what attacks are intended and make the necessary pre-emptive countermoves. Typical signals of an incoming punch are:

- A fist is suddenly clenched and shaking (the shaking is the physical expression of psychologically 'revving' up the power behind the punch).
- The fist is pulled backwards first to give it a longer travel and hence more power.
- There is a sharp intake of breath as the attacker fuels his body with oxygen prior to the punch. Alternatively, he may take many short, fast breaths as adrenaline alters his breathing.
- The puncher may make many small, fast steps on the spot as he tries to attain the correct targeting distance.
- The puncher will pull his eyebrows downwards in a subconscious attempt to protect the eyes from any return punches.

MAINTAIN STRONG EYE FOCUS

A proficient self-defence fighter will send out none of these signals. Practise throwing a punch straight from the guard position with no change in facial expression and no sudden breaths. Most crucially, the fist should go from where it is straight into the target without 'cocking'. From an open hand guard, just curl the hand into a fist and drive it straight forward. If all telegraphing signals are negated, the shock effect of your attacks is increased tremendously. Also, look directly where you are punching. Strong eye focus ensures correct targeting.

JAB WITH THE ELBOW

At very close range where punches are ineffective, switch to elbow techniques. The elbow is swung like a hook punch or an uppercut, or even a jab when thrust out to the side. The body dynamics of the techniques are exactly the same as the equivalent punches. Target points are the side of the head and the ribs. Tremendous leverage can be placed behind an elbow strike, and the hardness of the elbow itself only enhances the devastating results.

Punching is given lengthier consideration than other techniques in this chapter because of its primacy in a fight. Yet punching is far from self-sufficient. There are many more body weapons and strategies to hand.

KICKING

Spectacular kicking is regarded by many as the summit of fighting skill. In terms of practical self-defence, however, kicking can be more of a danger to the kicker if certain rules are not obeyed.

The first of these rules is unbreakable – do not kick at any target above the waist. Kicks below the waist are fast, difficult to catch, easy to control, and have a strong chance of impacting upon a vital target. Kicks above the waist have few promising targets. They are open to being grabbed and held by the recipient – once this happens, the kicker is easily pulled to the floor. Even if the above-waist kick is not held, the kicker can be shoved off-balance while perched precariously on one leg.

So, below-waist kicking is the rule. Below the navel is a target-rich environment. Vital points include the whole groin area, the outside of the thighs, the knees, the shins, and even the feet (when using stamping techniques).

A powerful shot to the groin can end a fight, but the value of most kicking techniques is to impose further pain distractions upon the opponent who is already beleaguered by your hand attacks. Kicks are also long-range techniques. They can be used to soften up or even defeat an opponent before punching range is reached.

Front snap kick

Kicking is an advanced and difficult skill, but one kick can be mastered to a useful degree by almost all – the front snap kick. This technique is similar to the simple action of kicking a ball, although with some crucial differences. The kick begins by lifting the knee of the kicking leg sharply upwards as high as it will go. From this point, the lower leg snaps outwards, violently sending the foot into the target. As the kick strikes, the hips are forced forwards to put body weight into the impact in much the same way as used in punching. These three stages are performed as one, the foot accelerating into the target from the moment it leaves the floor. The striking weapon is the ball of the foot, formed by pulling back the toes. If strong boots or shoes are worn, these will cope with most of the impact and indeed increase the pain factor. Aim to deliver the kick with the explosive force of a punch, not as a pushing technique. If kicking to the abdomen, aim for a point just behind the opponent's back and kick 'through' as if their body is not even in the way.

Front snap kick

Correct preparation for the front snap kick is vital if the kick is to generate decisive power. The knee of the kicking leg is raised strongly until the thigh is roughly parallel with the ground, while the lower leg is 'cocked' in readiness to deliver the kick.

The kicker must make a conscious effort not to raise his height during this phase, as the action directs some of the force of the kick upwards, rather than into the target.

Delivering a snap kick
Key rules of the front snap kick are as follows.

● During the delivery of the front snap kick, avoid bobbing up and down with the rhythm of the kick. The unnecessary body movement diverts some energy away from the straight line of the kick.
● Recover the leg with as much speed as you delivered it – time spent on one leg leaves you vulnerable to being knocked over or the leg grabbed.

The kick is delivered. The lower leg snaps forwards, the ball of the foot impacting squarely in the victim's lower torso, and the hips are pushed forwards to provide body weight. Note how the kicker maintains a good guard throughout the kick, ready to deliver hand techniques once the kicking leg returns to the ground. A kick to the lower torso will certainly produce pain. A direct blow to the groin can end a fight immediately. More serious injury can occur if any of the internal organs of the abdomen are torn or ruptured.

- Keep your guard up as you kick because you risk throwing yourself onto a heavy punch.
- Once the kick is made. keep fighting hard; don't stop to check on its results. The effect to strive for is a stunning speed strike which inflicts tremendous pain, not a heavy push.
- Practise the kick against kick bags and. particularly. strike shields. If you can shift a heavy training partner back a few feet with your kick, it is likely to have value.

Side thrust kick

The side thrust kick requires a high level of confidence and technique to perform correctly. Ideally, the opponent should be facing square on to provide a solid surface for the kicking foot to impact upon. To deliver the kick, the kicker twists sideways on to his opponent while raising one knee high into the air.

The leg is thrust out sideways into the opponent, hitting him hard in the abdomen and hopefully driving him backwards off his feet. The kicker must lean heavily into the kick to avoid knocking himself off-balance. If the opponent is very large and heavy, it is advisable not to attempt a side thrust kick unless you are of similar dimensions or can attack a vulnerable point such as knee or the groin.

Side thrust kick

More advanced techniques are the side thrust kick and roundhouse kick. You need competent tuition to acquire these as useful weapons, but they do provide useful attacking options. The side thrust kick is designed for vigorously pushing an opponent away or for executing a stamping attack to the groin, thighs, or knees.

It begins with the knee of the kicking leg lifting to the front as described in the previous technique. The body then uses the force of the lift to twist through 90 degrees. As the twist is made, the kicking leg is thrust out sideways into the target, the hip rolling over and adding its force behind the kick. The weapon is the sole of the foot or the edge of the foot. If executed properly with full body weight committed, the opponent may be propelled backwards by the force of the strike. If a knee is hit, the patella might shatter or knee dislocate.

Do not apply the side thrust kick it unless you have tried and tested it in every conceivable training scenario. Turned sideways and standing on one leg leaves you exposed. Do not lean backwards to get increased height into the kick; you risk overbalancing, so keep your torso upright and only kick to the limit of your flexibility. Do not use the kick against very heavy opponents if you are of slight build – your technique

is likely to have little pushing effect except on you, throwing you backwards.

The roundhouse kick

This is another advanced technique, but unlike the previous two kicks it begins by lifting the knee of the kicking leg high to the

Knee attack

Knees are useful weapons for attacking the side of the body, particularly the kidneys or lower rib areas.

They can also be driven into the opponent's thighs to create a 'dead leg' sensation and reduce his mobility.

Sweep throw

Here the man on the left grips his opponent's lapels and pulls the shoulders to the right to destabilize his opponent's balance. Simultaneously, the right leg sweeps the opponent's left leg from under him and crosses it in front of his body, taking him completely off-balance and hurling him to the ground.

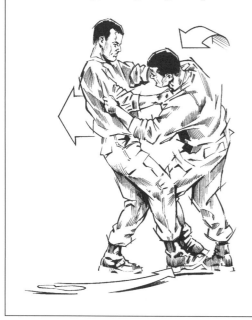

side of the body, the knee and foot held almost parallel to the ground. At the same time, the body spins through 90 degrees to point the knee at the target, before whipping out the lower leg to strike the opponent. The weapon is the ball of the foot (or toe of a heavy boot or shoe), but the shin bone is also used when attacking soft targets or at close range.

Roundhouse kicks are useful because they open up the side of the opponent's body. Thighs, knees, groin and abdomen can be attacked with the kick even if the opponent's body is turned at an angle. Similar cautions about using the roundhouse apply as the side thrust kick. It is a dynamic and powerful kicking technique, but one requiring diligent practice before it enters the practical repertoire.

FACE-TO-KNEE MOVE

Legs need not only be used for kicking techniques. Knee techniques offer a close-range resource. Drive the knee upwards directly into the opponent's groin area when fighting at close quarters. Alternatively, grip the opponent's neck or head with both hands and pull his face sharply downwards into your rising knee.

Stamping techniques are used to attack the feet. Toes and foot bones can be crushed with a heavy stamp; further pain is added by scraping the side of the boot down the shin bone before impacting upon the foot.

GRAPPLING AND THROWING

Martial artists from punching and kicking schools neglect grappling techniques at their peril. If an opponent does not go down under the first punches, he is likely to close the distance and begin grappling. It is a dangerous stage of the fight. The biggest danger is that you will be dragged to the ground in the scuffle, whereupon friends of the opponent will come to his aid with kicks against which you have little defence.

Certain elements of grappling come naturally, but grappling is still an advanced skill requiring professional training. Judo provides one of the best all-round groundings in grappling and throwing techniques, and some excellent judo techniques are illustrated and explained here. In any grappling contest, you should have one aim: the forced submission of your opponent.

Submission is achieved by: (1) injuring your opponent sufficiently to stop the fight; (2) imprisoning the opponent's limbs so that

he can no longer resist; or (3) applying a choke hold until the opponent loses consciousness. Described here are just a few of the more accessible techniques for achieving these aims.

GRAPPLE AND HEAD BUTT

When standing, grappling can be combined with other techniques. The head butt, for example, should begin with a strong grip to the opponent's collar or the back of his neck. The forehead is thrust forwards into the opponent's nose, face, or jaw, while the arms pull the opponent onto the technique to increase the impact.

Follow with a hip throw

Following such a stunning blow, the grip can be maintained and used in a basic hip throw. Holding on to the opponent's collar or the

Group attacks

One-on-one fights are increasingly becoming secondary to attacks by groups. Group assaults are terrifyingly serious. The psychology of group aggression means that the attacks are usually frenzied and frequently life-threatening. A single individual will always be at a tremendous disadvantage against a group. The best policy is to attack the second the group makes its move.

Try to take down the group's leader – usually the most vocal individual – with a violent technique straight away. This may dissuade the

rest of the group from attacking. If caught in an open area, move constantly to stop the group making a coordinated attack. Even better, find a place which restricts the group's attack options. Standing in the entrance to a narrow alleyway, the junction of two walls, or just inside an open door stops your attackers making a 360 degree assault pattern. They must come at you singly or in pairs, and so give you a much better fighting chance.

Lastly, try to find some sort of 'equalizer'. Improvised weapons are anything to hand

giving you an advantage. Keys are usually very accessible. They can make seriously effective knuckle-dusters if placed jutting out between the fingers. Any sort of stick or baton will also even the contest. When the group attacks the only policy is to fight in a frenzy, hitting and kicking every single target that presents itself. Group attackers long for compliant victims who they can kick to the ground. Someone resisting ferociously and inflicting injuries on the group can sap the group's confidence and lead them to break off the attack.

Throws

In this throw, the thrower uses an upward lift of the leg to lever his opponent off the ground and throw him forwards over his hip. Note, however, putting himself on one leg means that there is a strong likelihood of the thrower ending up on the ground with his opponent, so he must be confident of his ground-fighting techniques.

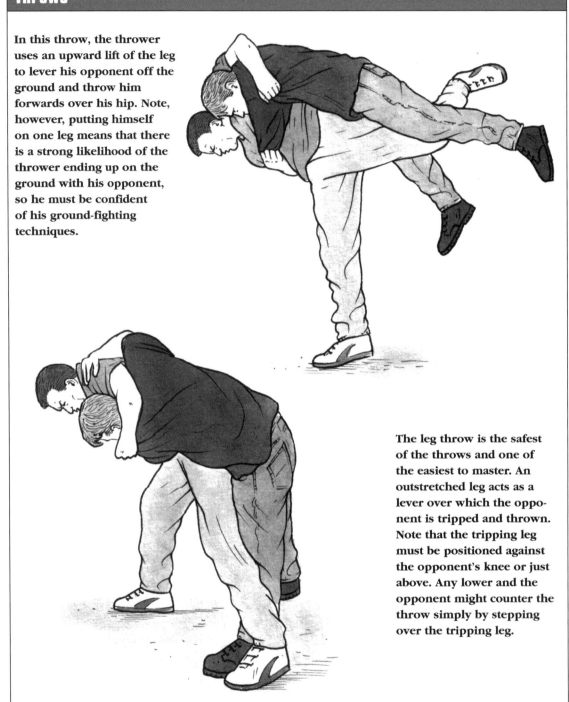

The leg throw is the safest of the throws and one of the easiest to master. An outstretched leg acts as a lever over which the opponent is tripped and thrown. Note that the tripping leg must be positioned against the opponent's knee or just above. Any lower and the opponent might counter the throw simply by stepping over the tripping leg.

top of his sleeves, step diagonally forwards with the right leg, passing it around the back of the opponent's right leg. Place the right hip against the opponent's right thigh. Push the opponent forcefully backwards using the arms, tripping him over your extended right leg while pushing upwards with your hip. Throw him hard to the ground, but try to keep your body as upright as possible to avoid overbalancing and following him down. Once he is on the ground, either make your escape or follow up with a finishing technique such as a stamp.

HANDS-FREE LEG SWEEP

A good way to down an opponent does not involve the arms at all. Leg sweeps are excellent long-range throw techniques and usually unexpected by your average street fighter. The aim of the sweep is to use your legs to drag the opponent's legs from under him.

To perform a basic sweep with the right leg, simply hook the right foot around the back of the opponent's left ankle. Pull and lift at the same time, dragging the opponent's leg from the floor and sweeping it up and to his right side. Performed with speed and violence, the sweep will often send the opponent sprawling onto the floor.

Apply extra force by grabbing the collar and pulling the opponent in the opposite direction to the sweep. Sweeps can be made in a multitude of directions using any available leg. Ideally, aim to sweep the opponent's front leg to the opposite side of his body. Maintain eye contact while performing the sweep. This distracts the opponent from

Scissor choke hold

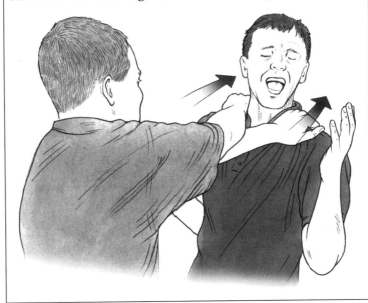

To use, cross the hands and grip the opponent's shoulders or collar, then pull the elbows forwards. The outer edges of the wrists should close tightly either side of the opponent's windpipe to make a dangerous throttle.

what is going on down below and stops you telegraphing your intentions.

A SIMPLE CHOKE HOLD

If a throw or sweep is not possible, a submission technique is usually required. Using a choke hold is perhaps your best option. This has its dangers – the vulnerability of the throat as a target is discussed earlier in this chapter – but being strangled will either panic your opponent into submission or render him unconscious and no longer a threat. From a frontal and standing position, a simple choke is applied by crossing your hands at the wrist, grabbing the opponent's collar, then using a scissor action to lever the wrists into the sides of the throat in a powerful strangle. Keep the opponent off-balance to stop him lashing out with his legs.

Rear strangle

The classic wrestler's half-nelson remains an excellent choke technique. Walking backwards while applying the choke lessens the opponent's ability to resist the strangle.

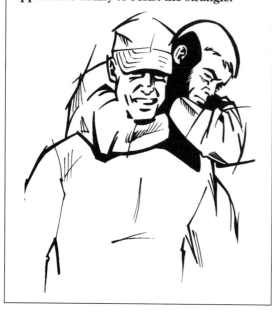

Choke hold from behind

A more stable choke hold uses the forearm and is applied to your opponent from the rear. For example, strike the opponent's left shoulder hard using the heel of the palm. His body is spun to the left. Immediately step forwards and behind the opponent. Hook the right arm around his throat, with the forearm pressing against the windpipe or carotid arteries either side. Place the right hand in the crook of the left elbow, and the left hand up around the back of the opponent's head. Lock the whole structure tight while pulling the opponent backwards off his feet to lessen resistance.

If the opponent suddenly goes limp and unconscious, immediately release the choke. The forearm choke is practical in a number of different scenarios and from different directions. If the elbow-lock structure cannot be made, simply link hands and apply the strangle using the force of both arms.

FINGER LOCK

Groundwork is the most dangerous element of grappling. For the inexperienced fighter struggling on the ground, the best recourse is to scratch, bite, struggle, punch, and kick with absolute ferocity at any available target. For those with more advanced skills, a lock can be used. Locks involve imprisoning a joint at the extremity of its movement and applying pressure to inflict pain and compliance. The most 'lockable' joints are those in the arms and fingers. The fingers are acutely sensitive to locks. Grab any finger and bend it back to its most extreme extent. Break the finger if necessary, especially if you are using the technique to free yourself from a choke hold. Keep twisting a locked finger to maintain the pressure and hopefully keep the opponent under control.

ARM LOCK

Locking arms is more difficult, as they are powered by strong muscle groups. Leverage against the elbow is always required. A simple lock begins when the opponent grabs your collar with his left hand in preparation for a right-hand punch. Grip the left hand strongly with your left hand, and swivel your body in an anticlockwise direction. Place the forearm of the right arm against the elbow of the opponent's left arm. Push hard using full body weight, locking the opponent's arm straight. Maintain the body twist while pushing down on the elbow, and the opponent can be controlled right down to ground level and held there. If engaged in ground fighting, try to lever the elbow against your knee or other unyielding surface to make the lock.

Caution is required when using locks against opponents on alcohol or drugs. Such individuals have numbed pain receptors, making them almost oblivious to the pain inflicted by a heavy lock. Many will not know they are injured until they awake from their intoxication the next day. Be prepared for this eventuality, and adopt different techniques – particularly punches aimed at a knockout blow – to resolve the fight.

FIGHT DYNAMICS AND DEFENDING

The basic secret of self-defence is encapsulated in this command: 'Attack first, attack hard, keep attacking.' 'Hit first' might sound unethical, but it is demanded. Whoever receives the first hard blow to the face is likely to lose the fight. Try to make sure that it is not you. Buy yourself a striking opportunity with some elementary psychological warfare. As the opponent strides in, ask him a question such as 'What's your dad doing these days?' or 'How's the family?' The question will create a fractional pause for thought. In this moment, strike hard.

'Attack hard' sounds obvious, but it is worth reinforcing. Do not be afraid of unleashing the full power of your techniques.

Many people are rightly worried about the legal consequences of seriously hurting an attacker, but keep in mind the old saying: 'It is better to be judged by twelve than carried by six.' Restraining techniques will only give the attacker an advantage, and he is unlikely to show you the same mercy as you are showing him. So put every ounce of power behind techniques and save yourself before worrying about possible repercussions.

'Keep attacking' means seeing the fight through to its end. When adrenaline is running high, people are extraordinarily resistant to pain. A single technique is often not enough to finish a fight. Instead, continual attacks should be prosecuted until the opponent is thoroughly defeated through submission, injury, or knockout. Beware of an opponent's sudden inexplicable surrender. Stay on your guard and control him with a strong voice in case he is simply regaining strength for another attack. If you are injured, do not display your weakness – it will usually encourage the opponent to attack harder. Keep fighting to the best of

Handling fear

During an assault fear can almost paralyse the body with shakes, nausea, mental withdrawal and disbelief. Yet if managed properly, fear will provide the energy to fight hard, move fast and resist pain. Here are some key techniques for making fear an ally rather than an enemy:

● Counter every negative internal statement with a positive one. For example, if your mind says 'I can't

handle this' consciously contradict it by saying 'I'm completely in control'. The process will feel artificial but it can have surprisingly effective results.

● Act out the role of a confident street fighter. Psychological studies have shown that mental states usually take their lead from external behaviour rather than the other way round. Literally act confident by standing straight and strong,

controlling the voice, breathing deeply but steadily, and maintaining eye contact with the opponent. Though you may feel fearful internally, the play acting will give you a greater degree of control.

● Breathe properly. Pull in deep breaths to give your muscles the requisite oxygen for the fight. The breaths will also steady your mind and help you to think more clearly about your defence.

Ground defence

The priority in ground defence is to protect the torso and head from kicking techniques. Here the man on the ground raises his knees to form a protective barrier to the torso, while the arms shield the head.

The aim of a ground defence should be to keep the feet and legs pointing towards those of the attacker. In this position, the defender can kick out at his opponent's shins, knees, and groin, hopefully buying enough time to get to his feet.

your ability and, if possible, choose more decisive vital points as your targets.

STAY ON YOUR FEET

While fight is in progress, be careful with footwork. Move using short, shuffling steps within the guard position, and resist crossing your legs and becoming unbalanced. Under all circumstances, avoid falling to the floor. If you do find yourself there, curl up and cover your head with your arms. Your priority is to regain a standing position. Your attacker will almost invariably start kicking you. Twist your body so that you can kick out with your legs at his shins, knees, and groin. The moment you hurt him and buy yourself a second's respite, try to spring to your feet in order to resume the fight.

KEEP YOUR GUARD UP

A ground defence raises the point of defensive techniques in general. Many self-defence manuals include large sections on blocking techniques. In most cases, they do more harm than good. Actively blocking a punch or kick breaks your guard unnecessarily, and risks damaging the blocking limb itself. By far the better option is completely to avoid the attacks in the first place, while maintaining a good guard to protect the face and chest.

SHARPEN YOUR REFLEXES

Watch your attacker intently. The best place to stare is at the sternum – from here, your peripheral vision will take in all the

Blocking

Of limited use in a real fight, blocking can be used to ward off lighter blows or break grips. Blocks are made with the forearm in a circular motion across the body. The hip corresponding to the blocking arm should be pushed in the direction of the block to increase force.

movements. If a punch is launched, snap the head rapidly out of the way using a strong reflex action from the waist. To defend against kicks, move diagonally either side of the opponent, pushing hard off the legs to get out of the way before the kick makes contact. If either a punch or kick does make contact – as it surely will in a vigorous fight – make sure it hits nowhere vital. Take punches on your guard and quickly raise one leg against the kick to protect the abdomen.

Knife attack

Even the most highly trained defence expert is at a disadvantage when faced by an assailant with a knife. At very close ranges, they are more lethal than even a gun – knives never run out of ammunition. Knives cut or puncture on contact, and even a wound to the arm or leg can be fatal. Here are some basic procedures for trying to deal with a knife attacker:

● Wrapping a jacket or thick piece of clothing around the forearm will give some protection to the arm during an encounter. Use the protected arm to swipe away the attacks and your other other limbs to attack.

● Upgrade the selection of body targets to the most vulnerable. The throat and eyes both become legitimate targets. As soon as the opportunity arises, attack with extreme violence, preferably while gripping and controlling the attacker's knife hand.

● Find an improvised weapon to equalize the odds. A stick or club is preferable. Direct blows at the knife hand itself and also against the elbow joints to deaden the arm. When using a stick, rest it on your shoulder ready to strike and out of reach of the attacker should he try to grab it.

● If the attacker is just using the knife to threaten as part of a mugging, always give him your wallet or purse if this will send him away.

Discussing the mechanics of self-defence is not pleasant. The techniques and mentality described here may seem slightly crude and even thuggish, but you must remind yourself that those who perpetrate violence seldom show mercy, even if the victim is unconscious.

GUNS AND SELF-DEFENCE

Some countries permit the carrying of concealed handguns as a form of self-defence. The policy is a controversial one. Some claim it dissuades criminals from violence, others say it merely adds to gun-related crime. Whatever the arguments, if you are going to carry a handgun, bear in mind the following:

● Get proper training for using your handgun, and train regularly in correct technique.
● Make sure that you have a proper licence for the concealed firearm, and check your licence is still valid if you cross state or national borders.
● Have the gun properly secured about your person in a holster, not slipped into a pocket. Be aware of potentially catching the trigger or hammer of the gun on your clothing when you withdraw it.
● In the United States, around 48,000 people are killed every year by firearms. The majority of those are killed in firearms accidents. Keep the gun in a locked cabinet while at home, particularly if there are children in the house.
● If you are called upon to use your gun in self-defence, be deliberate in your actions. Try to stop the assailant first with a verbal warning. Order him to lie down slowly on the floor, keeping his eyes on your face and his hands clearly visible. If you have to open fire, aim only for the centre of the attacker's chest – you are likely to miss any smaller targets. When using a powerful magnum handgun, be aware of where your bullet will travel should it pass straight through the opponent.
● Immediately after a shooting incident, put your gun on safety and put it away – otherwise you increase your risk of being mistakenly shot if you are still holding the gun when the police arrive.

Patterns of violent injury

In the year 2000 1,021,118 males and 650,361 females were treated in US emergency departments for non-fatal violence-related incidents. A massive 81 per cent of these injuries resulted from blows inflicted either by body-weapon means (usually fist or foot, but including head, elbows, and knees) or via an improvised clubbing or striking weapon.

Knife wounds accounted for 8 per cent and gunshots a relatively low 3 per cent, although the injuries resulting from these instruments were often extremely serious. As indicated by the gender breakdown, men in the 18–35 age

category were at greater risk of being attacked. The physical nature of the injuries fell into six main categories: contusions (31 per cent), lacerations (23 per cent), fractures (10 per cent), internal injuries (7 per cent), puncture wounds (7 per cent), and strains or sprains (7 per cent). The head received 54 per cent of injuries, while the arms/hands and upper trunk took 19 and 10 per cent, respectively.

Statistical data from Centers for Disease Control and Prevention, Morbidity and Mortality Weekly Report (31 May 2002)

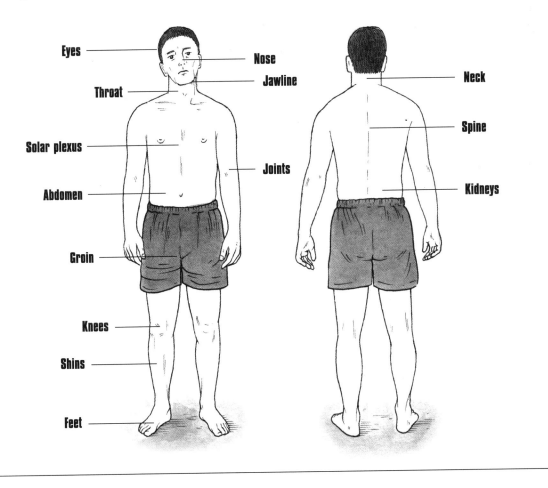

Eyes
Nose
Jawline
Throat
Solar plexus
Abdomen
Joints
Groin
Knees
Shins
Feet

Neck
Spine
Kidneys

CHAPTER FIVE

Transport security and safety

Almost all modes of travel raise the stakes regarding the risk of accident and injury. Travel also brings us into direct contact with potentially threatening strangers.

Density, unpredictability, and criminally minded opportunists characterize the urban environment. Perhaps such typically urban characteristics are at their most apparent when we navigate the city, crossing unfamiliar neighbourhoods and straying far from our locale. Moreover, we may find ourselves travelling across the city far from street level – underground – using city subway systems notorious for high crime rates and especially hazardous by night. On isolated train platforms and in lonely walkways late at night, we must be remember to be especially on the lookout for potential threats.

REMAIN ALERT WHEN TRAVELLING

Maintaining a streetwise attitude throughout your journey across the city is of paramount importance. Even as commonplace a journey as our daily commute entails risk, and, by failing to observe the rules of basic street-wise behaviour, we may inadvertently make ourselves more vulnerable to criminal intent than we realize. Knowing what to look for when travelling can help you to anticipate criminal or threatening behaviour before you find yourself falling victim to it.

DRIVING RISKS

By contrast, the protective shell of a private vehicle may seem a much safer way to cross the city. Yet our feelings of security inside our car are greatly exaggerated, especially given the rise of new gang-initiated crimes such as carjacking. Driving may present certain obvious dangers, but we are also at risk every time we park our car and walk to and from it, particularly if we fail to choose a parking location wisely. Moreover, the very mobility we enjoy in our cars can work against us. Launching into a badly planned journey can lead us into neighbourhoods in which gang activities can quickly overwhelm. An often territorial and aggressive environment, the road can be a place of sudden unexpected violence. Even the most everyday route entails the risk of encountering a road rager.

FEELING SAFE IN THE AIR

Living in an urban environment makes travel by subway or by car almost inevitable, and, when most city transport systems are under-funded and underpatrolled, and when the ratio of law enforcement officers to citizens is not always sufficiently high, it is our responsibility to be protect ourselves by maintaining a defensive attitude. Air travel is now almost as common as taking the train once was, but, for all its familiarity, it remains an environment in which security and health considerations are especially life-threatening. It can present us with sometimes dangerous weather conditions that airlines are not always able to predict or detect in advance. Most airlines are disinclined to spell out to us exactly why keeping our seat belts on at all times is so important. Knowing what to expect and how best to deal with the frightening experience of extreme turbulence

is essential to our survival. Similarly, as the number of air rage incidents increase, and because air travel can trigger psychotic reactions in the mentally unstable, knowing how to react in such an emergency situation can only serve to boost our confidence and feelings of security when we travel.

VEHICLE SECURITY

This is best approached from a variety of different perspectives, ranging from the car's maintenance and overall performance, to our parking choices and our preparedness in the event of an accident or vehicle fire.

Essential security equipment and fittings

Clearly we are at our most vulnerable during a breakdown, when we may be forced to wait for emergency services in an unknown neighbourhood. It is very evident that preventing breakdown is the number-one key to our safety and security when using a vehicle. Keeping your car in good running order should therefore be taken extremely seriously.

You should know your car and its parts and their functions well, and you should inwardly digest and regularly consult the set of guidelines for routine maintenance that your car's manufacturer recommends. Many of us tend to put off or neglect seemingly non-essential maintenance work. Yet routine checks recommended by the car manufacturer are vital to the car's upkeep and should never be ignored. Brakes and wheel alignment must be routinely checked because either could make your vehicle stall or fail to stop, causing serious risk of accident and injury. The tyres, the car's electric system (meaning the alternator, headlights, brake lights, and so on), cooling system (including the water pump), timing chain or cam belt, and catalytic converter and exhaust or muffler should also be regularly checked. A faulty catalytic converter can block the exhaust system and progressively kill the engine. A faulty exhaust pipe can gradually leak carbon monoxide into the car. Leaks or faults in either can lead to a vehicle fire.

Plan ahead for the road

In the event of a breakdown, you should always be prepared, with an up-to-date emergency insurance plan that includes emergency assistance across the country. Keeping a fully charged cell phone in the car at all times in order to call for help is an excellent measure that will help you to avoid interacting with strangers in the search for a telephone. Your spare tyre should be kept full of air, and you should know how to replace it yourself. The car itself should be kitted out with a first-aid kit, bottled water, and an emergency kit, including reflective materials in case you break down at night.

Fit secure locks

In addition to ensuring basic overall car maintenance, equipping the car with fundamental security devices will greatly enhance your safety by deterring would-be thieves and attackers. Most important are the exterior locks on your car. These should never be handles that can be grabbed and pulled. If your car has these type of T-shaped door style of lock, they should be immediately replaced with straight locks that will not permit a thief or attacker a firm hold. Vehicles with central locking systems are the most secure because a would-be attacker or thief is less able to jump into the car as you are locking or unlocking it. Ideally, your car should be equipped with an intrusion alarm system and a two-way radio or a radio telephone.

Steering wheel lock

This anti-theft device is used by many drivers to deter car thieves. Your steering wheel lock should be made of steel.

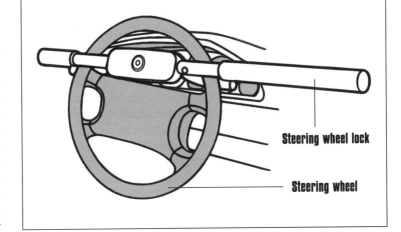

Steering wheel lock

Steering wheel

Pedal jack

The pedal jack is another anti-theft device, one which locks and blocks the brake and accelerator pedals, immobilizing both.

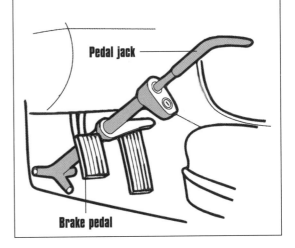

Pedal jack

Brake pedal

Reveal no personal details

Critically, the keys to the car should never feature any form of identification. Should your car keys be stolen, your car could also be stolen and your address would be made known to potential criminal opportunists. You should never leave your car running with the key in the ignition, and never leave any trace of your identity inside the car. Should you lose your ignition key, have the ignition switch changed immediately.

Ensuring that your car radio is as invisible as possible is the best way to prevent attracting thieves to the car. As car radios are one of the biggest sources of attraction to the would-be thief or attacker, a superior security fitting is a slide-mount removable radio device that you can take with you when you leave the car.

Additional deterrents

A steering wheel lock is an essential piece of equipment for deterring thieves. This prevents the steering wheel from turning, and its high visibility has been proven to deter theft. Fitting the car with a key-operated or hidden manual switch that interrupts the power supply from the battery to the ignition, or an ignition cut-off key, is an excellent additional security measure. Similarly, a fuel cut-off device is available that prevents the flow of petrol or gas once the fuel in the gas line is used.

An ignition column guard that protects the ignition starting system, fitting around the steering column and over the ignition starting system, is another recommended security fitting. Preventing access to the power source, battery, or siren can be achieved by using a secondary bonnet or hood lock, to back up the main lock. Similarly, a secondary locking device installed inside the trunk which is key-operated will protect valuables in the boot or trunk, and will prevent a would-be attacker or thief from slipping into the car undetected. A guard plate over the boot or trunk lock affords additional protection to the trunk cylinder.

Safe driving in urban areas

When driving through unfamiliar urban areas, be aware at all times of both other drivers and the movements of pedestrians on the street. Be especially wary of any pedestrian in the middle of the road, even if they appear to be selling flowers or newspapers, or some other commodity. Never allow your car windows to be washed by those offering such services at stoplights. Keep your doors locked and your windows rolled up, and be particularly alert when drawing up to a stop sign or red light or crossing. Avoid giving directions from your car, and never roll your window down to a stranger, who might grab you and put a gun to your head.

Car safety essentials

- Replace handle-shaped locks with straight locks on car doors.
- Use a wheel lock, and conceal your car radio and other valuables.
- Never use identification on your ignition key.
- Never leave your key in the ignition.
- Check your spare tyre regularly for air pressure.
- Learn how to change a tyre yourself.
- Always keep your cell phone charged up in the car at all times when you are driving.
- Carry a first-aid kit, reliable flashlight, a fix-a-flat tyre kit, electrical tape, bottled water, and a white handkerchief, flares, or reflective triangles in the car for use in emergencies.

Parking safety

Plan parking carefully. Parking in front of a skip or dumpster gives too much cover to opportunists who may leap out from behind them as you are unlocking your car. Park in well-lit areas close to shopping areas and avoid lonelier spots.

What to do if hit from behind

When driving, watch carefully for signs of distraction tactics in other drivers, who may be attempting to surround you as part of an organized robbery. In particular, you should be aware of so-called 'bump and rob' scams. This term refers to when another car purposely drives into the back of your car in order to force you out of your car in response. Should you get out of your car at this point, you are very likely to be robbed at gun or knifepoint, and to have your car stolen on the spot.

If you are hit from behind, no matter how upset you may be, or eager to take down the other driver's details, you should instead immediately call the police, using a cellular phone. Be sure to decline any offers of help from the other vehicle or from bystanders until the police arrive. If you do not have a phone, remain inside your car, with the doors locked and windows rolled up. You should avoid conversation with the person who drove into the back of your car.

Do not offer assistance

Similarly, you should never stop to offer assistance to a broken-down car by the roadside, as this is often another ruse to facilitate robbery. If you are concerned about

Parking safety

- Try to park close to open businesses that you could run into, if threatened.
- Park in well-lit places, and anticipate your return to the car after nightfall.
- Lock your car every time you leave it, even when it is parked in a locked garage.
- Never park between two vans or trucks, where you cannot be seen getting in or out of your vehicle.
- Choose car parks operated by an attendant.
- Avoid parking near alleyways or in large, under-used car parks.
- Ask friends or co-workers to walk you to your car whenever possible.
- When you walk alone to your car, walk briskly and confidently, keeping your head up to deter any would-be attackers.
- Have your car key ready, with the door key protruding from between your index and middle fingers to be used as a defensive weapon and to ensure you can enter your car quickly.
- Always look in the back seat and on floor of your vehicle through the window before you get in.
- Always lock the doors once you are inside.
- Use a personal alarm to attract attention if you are attacked.
- Have your cell phone programmed for automatic emergency dial.

the breakdown, call the police and give them a map reference and directions to the breakdown so that they can investigate and offer assistance.

Call the police if you are followed

If you find yourself being followed when driving through an urban area, avoid panicking. First, make sure that the car simply is not simply going in the same direction as you. If you decide that you are being followed, call the police at the earliest opportunity, using a cellular phone and without taking your eyes off the road. If you do not have a cellular phone, drive through the window of a drive-by fast-food establishment and ask them to phone the police or drive to a police station.

Think ahead when parking

Never park thoughtlessly, as merely for the sake of convenience you could be putting yourself needlessly at risk. However hurried you may be, you should always think ahead when parking. Never park anywhere that may be concealed from view or that affords shadowy spaces that could hide an attacker.

When parking by day, bear in mind that you may not be returning to your car until nightfall, and park close to street lighting or businesses that will be open. Always leave and approach your car with extreme caution, remaining alert and watchful and checking the car carefully before entering it, in case anyone may be hiding around, underneath, or even inside the vehicle.

Planning safe routes

Planning a safe route is largely a matter of common sense and a case of avoiding bad neighbourhoods known for high crime rates. Route planning also means knowing where you are going, so that you do not inadvertently end up lost in such a neighbourhood. When driving, avoid turning into or parking in dead ends or no-outlet streets, streets that run across empty lots or by warehouses, or streets that run alongside abandoned docks or along waterfronts of any kind.

Read your local newspaper and learn where gang activity and crime hot spots are concentrated. If you must pass through a dangerous neighbourhood, choose the fastest and quickest method possible – preferably an expressway or a main road with as few stop signs and lights as possible.

Preventing carjacking

Carjacking is a crime of opportunity, undertaken primarily by gangs in order to raise fast cash. Such gangs prey on obvious targets in the street, and your car may constitute a mobile lure. Using an advanced alarm system and locking device can deter car thieves that operate on empty parked cars, but carjackers are more sinister and will target cars *and* their drivers. Carjackers will stalk you and will seize the moment to take possession after singling you out.

The surest way to avoid carjacking is to prevent it happening – to plan safe routes and to avoid the situations vulnerable to attack. A carjacking can occur anytime, but it is far more likely to occur late at night, to a lone driver who is lost or driving through an unfamiliar neighbourhood.

Avoiding carjacking
● Avoid driving alone, particularly at night.
● Keep the car doors and windows locked at all times.

Road rage

If you encounter an angry driver, never get out of your car or risk getting into an argument, even a verbal one. Call the police to the scene on a cell phone, or drive to the nearest police station and allow the police to mediate the situation.

What carjackers look for

- Intersections controlled by stoplights or signs
- Garages and subway/rail-connection parking areas, shopping malls, and grocery stores.
- Self-service gas (petrol) stations and car washes.
- Drive-through ATMs (automated teller machines).
- Residential driveways and streets where there are people constantly getting into and out of cars
- Highway exit and entry ramps, or any other place where drivers have to slow their speed or stop

---

- Drive in the middle lane to make your car harder to approach when slowing down.
- Beware of 'bump and rob' scams.
- Never stop to assist anyone on the street – call the police instead of getting out of your car.
- If someone tells you that you have a flat tyre or that your engine is on fire, do not get out to look until you are well away from this stranger and are in a well-populated safe area or garage.
- Be aware when you slow down at ATMs, on ramp exits, and at stoplights.

Defending against carjacking

Falling prey to carjackers can be a terrifying experience. Ultimately, your life is worth more than your car; if a gun is used, give up your car and obey the carjackers' instructions. Trying to make a fast getaway in the car

could prove extremely dangerous or even fatal because, should you lose control of the car, you could end up in worse trouble or find yourself being shot at.

If you are forced to leave your vehicle at gunpoint, try to stay calm, remembering the key principles of survival on the street, avoiding conflict and antagonism, and obeying all instructions. As soon as the carjackers have left with your car, concentrate on getting away from the immediate neighbourhood as safely as possible. Avoid those who may seem to be seeking to help you as they may be other gang members or other opportunists looking to rob you.

DEALING WITH ROAD RAGE

Road rage is a widely publicized syndrome whereby drivers attack other drivers on the road as a result of outbursts of extreme anger at common driving mistakes or mishaps. Road rage is not criminally motivated as such, yet can result in criminally violent action or even murder as 'pumped-up' drivers lose control and lash out mindlessly. In other words, road rage is usually out of proportion to the incident and is an exaggerated reaction of unpredictable force.

You should be aware of the signs of road rage and of its potential for serious or even fatal consequences. Sudden roadside stabbings, beatings with heavy objects, and throttling are some of the worst outcomes of road rage frenzies. Murders have taken place even with witnesses such as partners or family members desperately trying to protect their loved one. Because the

What to do in a carjacking attempt

- Never argue if the carjacker threatens you with a gun or other weapon – give up your car.
- Get away from the area as quickly as possible.
- Try to remember what the carjacker looked like – sex, race, age, hair and eye details, special features, clothes.
- Report the crime to the police immediately.

Aggressive driving

You should avoid making angry gestures when driving. Remember that your behaviour could contribute to a road rage attack.

consequences of road rage can be so dire, the slightest hint of the behaviour associated with it should be motivation for extreme caution.

Saying 'Sorry' helps

Research has shown that road ragers most often become upset because of accidental or unintentional mistakes on the road made by other drivers. If you find yourself under verbal attack for cutting in front of a road rager, or some other 'misdemeanor', one of the responses most widely recommended is a clear apology. Do not, however, risk rolling down the window. It is suggested by many police departments and experts that you instead keep a sign in your car boldly marked 'Sorry' that you can hold up for view and that will be visible through your car window. Research has shown that most road ragers will give up their angry behaviour at this point, as though the act of communicating the message 'sorry' alone jolts them into regaining some emotional control. However, even after indicating that you are sorry, keep your distance; do not leave the car, and do not engage in any kind of interaction.

Road rage dos and don'ts

- Stay in your car.
- Call the police if you feel threatened.
- NEVER respond with an angry gesture or action.
- Keep a 'Sorry' sign on hand in the car to show to the other driver through a rolled-up window.
- Remain inside your car with your windows rolled up and your doors locked, and do not leave your vehicle until the police arrive.
- Do not attempt to talk your way out of the situation.

If your car or their car has been hit and you need to make or provide insurance claims, call the police on your cellular phone, and do not attempt to begin negotiations with the other driver. Even if the other driver appears to have calmed down initially, his mood may be volatile and unpredictable.

COPING WITH ROAD TRAFFIC ACCIDENTS

Most of us will experience a traffic accident at some point in our lives. While any accident, however minor, is always unsettling, a more serious accident can lead to lasting or permanent trauma. When an accident occurs, most drivers and passengers are too shocked to think clearly. Yet reacting swiftly and taking immediate precautions may make vital and life-saving differences to a traumatic situation.

As soon as you have assessed the situation for immediate danger, you should assess any casualties. In particular, look for anyone who may be trapped; for example, a child under a car or anyone inside the car. If you need to help an injured passenger or driver who cannot move, or who may be trapped in the vehicle, approach them with extreme caution. Never wrench open the door because casualties may have become impaled on a door or somehow trapped within sharply twisted metal. Take extreme care if you insert your head through a window, and beware of sharp metal and broken glass at all times.

Assess any casualties for bleeding, burns, fractures, or other injuries. Do not touch any burns or put any fabric or material over them. Use a cellular phone to call the police and emergency services, or, if you do not have a cellular phone, ask passers-by or flag down traffic from a safe distance and demand help.

You should never move any injured person from the vehicle unless there is a risk of fire or unless their breathing is blocked by the position they are in. Comfort casualties verbally, reassure them that help is on its way, put extra clothing or blankets over them to keep them warm and to help ease shock symptoms, and wait for the ambulance to arrive. Do not allow the 'walking wounded' to stray from the scene, and keep all children under control and away from oncoming traffic.

Shivering, shaking, crying, and feeling faint are all normal reactions to an accident, but full-blown shock can be fatal, and you should watch carefully for any sign of this. Severe shock should be treated as an

Road accident checklist

- Are any of the vehicles likely to roll or move?
- Is there spilt fuel or any fire hazard present?
- Is either vehicle in contact with a power line or anything else that could cause an electric shock or explosion?
- If a truck or van is involved, is the load safe or likely to collapse?
- Is anyone smoking, which could cause an explosion?

What to do in cases of severe shock

- Keep the victim warm.
- If there are no serious apparent injuries, raise the victim's feet higher than his or her head.
- Loosen clothing and take a pulse.
- Make sure that the victim's air passages are open, and ensure a supply of fresh air.
- If breathing and a pulse are absent, you may need to start CPR.
- Avoid unnecessary noise and questions.
- Give only small amounts of water or none at all: if there is any sign of an abdominal injury, do not give water.
- Never give alcohol or caffeine.
- Continue to monitor breathing and pulse until help arrives.

emergency situation, and it is very important to be able to determine the signs that distinguish it from lesser forms of shock.

Signs of serious shock

Look for the following primary signs of shock in any major injury or other medical emergency:

- Cold, clammy, pale or mottled skin
- Weak and rapid pulse
- Lightheadedness or fainting
- Irregular, rapid, and shallow breathing
- Chills
- Extreme thirst

Other possible signs of shock include:

- Pinched and vacant expression
- Glassy or dull eyes, with enlarged pupils and a staring gaze
- Restlessness, agitation, or groaning without experiencing pain or exhibiting obvious injuries
- Loss of bowel or bladder control

Crash injuries

Although you should never attempt to treat injuries, being aware of them can be helpful. Certain types of impact are associated with certain injuries: side impact often leads to a fractured upper leg (femur) and/or lower leg on the side of impact and may also cause a fractured pelvis, a shoulder or upper arm injury on the side of impact, and a possible head injury. High-speed impact usually causes severe internal bleeding, multiple fractures, impacted pelvis, head and spinal injuries, and multiple lacerations. You should be aware of the rapid deterioration in unconscious casualties with head injuries.

Impact from behind

Rear-end collisions usually cause cervical spine injuries ('whiplash' effect) and facial injuries. Ejection from the vehicle most often leads to head and spinal injuries, unconsciousness, multiple fractures, multiple lacerations to top of body and head, and internal bleeding. Roll over cases, where the car turns over, can cause a number of different injuries and particularly affects children who are even less well protected by seat belts than adults.

Motorcycle, bicycle, and pedestrian accidents

Coming off a motorcycle at speed causes riders to suffer fractures of the femur, wrist and ankle fractures, head injuries, and deceleration injuries resulting in severe internal bleeding. NEVER remove the motorcyclist's helmet unless the airway is obstructed or the casualty is not breathing because damage to the neck and spine can be fatal or paralysing. Bicycle accidents usually cause cyclists multiple fractures, multiple lacerations, and head injuries.

Pedestrians are more often 'run under' rather than 'run over', as they are thrown off their feet by the impact. Most will suffer a range of side impact injuries. Head and spinal injuries are also common, especially where the casualty's head has struck the vehicle's bonnet or windshield. Small children may be 'run over' and still be under the vehicle when it stops.

MAKING AN ACCIDENT ZONE SAFE

The next rapid consideration should be oncoming traffic. If there are no serious injuries, the drivers should move their cars to the side of the road and out of the way of oncoming traffic as soon as possible. Leaving cars parked in the middle of the road or at a busy intersection could result in an even more serious accident. If a car cannot be moved, drivers and passengers should remain in the cars with seat belts fastened until help arrives. The hazard lights should be turned on, and, if either car has cones, flares, or warning triangles on board, these items should be used to ward off oncoming traffic.

Take charge of the situation

Traffic accidents are all too often followed by erratic behaviour, typical of those in shock. It is important to try to keep calm, to attempt to calm others, and to exchange the following information: name, address, phone number, insurance company, policy number, driver licence number and licence plate number for the driver and the owner of each vehicle. It is also essential to obtain a written description of each car, including year, make, model, and colour, and to make full notes on the accident and how each of you believe it occurred. If you have a camera, document as much as possible about the accident. File an accident report immediately, and check your insurance plan.

Vehicle fire precautions

- Regularly check the hoses, gaskets, and fittings on your engine for any leaks or cracks.
- Place a multipurpose accessible and visibly located fire extinguisher in your car.
- Maintain your car regularly and act promptly on repairs.
- Never flick cigarette ash out of an open window – use the car's ashtray.
- Equip your car with a fire extinguisher and know how to use it.
- Never lift the car's hood/bonnet to inspect the fire – flames could engulf you.
- Avoid inhaling fumes from the car when it is on fire – move away.

Road accidents dos and don'ts

- Avoid touching the injured.
- DO NOT move any seriously injured casualties from the vehicle unless there is a risk of fire or further collision, or airway protection, control of severe bleeding, or CPR are necessary.
- Do not cover or attempt to dress burns.
- Do not give water to the injured.
- Never remove a motorcyclist's or cyclist's helmet or move any injured person's head or neck.
- Be watchful for serious shock symptoms and take them very seriously.
- Reassure the injured and use your voice to calm them.

Handling vehicle fires

Although relatively rare, such fires can be fatal because all vehicles are highly flammable and, when burning, give off extreme heat and harmful gases. Vehicles on fire are also likely to explode. The larger the vehicle's fuel tank, the more serious the damage from a vehicle fire is likely to be. Faulty exhaust pipes, or mufflers, can leak fuel and start a fire in dry grass that can spread to the vehicle. Smelling exhaust fumes inside your car is a sure sign of a serious leak in the exhaust system and should prompt you to seek immediate repair. Another sign of an exhaust leak is a 'putt putt' sound coming from parts of the exhaust other than its normal outlet when the car is running. The source could be a rust hole or a crack caused by hitting uneven road surfaces. If the car is burning an unusually high amount of fuel, or if its performance seems in any way slowed or irregular, have it checked by a professional.

Remain alert

Never allow yourself to fall asleep on public transport. Not only will you be vulnerable to pickpockets and other opportunists or deviants, but you are more likely to depart from your planned route as well. Read a book or newspaper to keep yourself awake.

Another major cause of vehicle fires is an overheated catalytic converter, part of the car's exhaust system. This is a very high temperature heat source that can ignite if it comes into contact with flammable materials. If your car is fitted with a catalytic converter, be mindful of the high temperatures it can reach and of its potential for causing fire.

What to do if the vehicle is on fire

A vehicle on fire can be an extremely alarming experience, but the first rule in the event of a fire is to stay calm. Swerving suddenly off the

Avoid shortcuts

Subway stations can be confusing, but taking shortcuts through lonely, underused tunnels should be avoided wherever possible.

road or sudden braking could result in injury, or worse, and you should never suddenly stop the car in the middle of the road.

If the hood/bonnet or dashboard begins smoking, check the road, pull over, and turn off the engine. Get out of the car, move quickly to a safe distance, and call emergency services. NEVER raise the hood/bonnet of the car if you see flames: a fire in the engine could flare up, causing you serious burns. If you have a fire extinguisher in your car, poke its nozzle through the front grill and spray the engine area thoroughly to quell the fire, then wait for the fire department at a safe distance from your car.

Smoking in your car, especially if it is full of litter and trash, is an obvious hazard and should be avoided. If you must smoke inside the car, use the ashtray provided, and make sure that cigarettes are properly extinguished.

TRAINS AND SUBWAYS

Public transport is fraught with potential dangers and risks, and, as with any urban situation, maintaining a confident, alert appearance should be your first rule. Your journey by public transport will entail a series of unfolding, shifting situations as passengers embark and disembark, and as you yourself change trains and plan your route. Think carefully before you commit yourself to a train car, and pay close attention to those getting on and off, watching for any sudden jostling or grabbing, or for any other signs of organized crime or threat. Paying attention to evident signs of mental instability in individuals is also very important, and you should avoid travelling alone with any passenger who seems inebriated or who is showing signs of obvious mental health issues that could be threatening.

SECURITY ON LATE-NIGHT SUBWAYS

Late-night subway travel is often a necessary evil – when returning late from work, from an airport, or from a downtown event where

Stay with the crowd

Always avoid isolated parts of the platform, and stay close to groups of people when waiting for your train.

car travel has not been possible. Many subway systems are underpoliced and provide a haven for crimes such as pick-pocketing and robbery. Robbery can be accompanied by intimidation and violence, and rape is another extreme menace.

Attacks can take place on unmanned train carriages between subway stops or even at the stops themselves. The area around subway stops is often a hot spot for late-night crimes such as rape, robbery, and carjacking, and being on guard at all times, especially along tunnels and walkways, is essential if you are to make it safely home.

PERSONAL SECURITY ABOARD CROWDED TRAINS

You may be forced to board a crowded train during rush hour. Before you get onto the train, be sure that your wallet or purse is concealed, preferably in an inside front jacket pocket. If you are carrying your purse or valuables in a bag, make sure that the opening of the bag hangs close to your chest, within view. For example, if you have a backpack, take it off your back and hold it to your chest instead.

Avoid revealing anything that might attract interest or that might give away your

Watch exits

Note who gets on and off the train, and survey the platform through the exit door before you leave the train yourself.

Subway security

- Never fall asleep – always remain alert.
- Never enter an empty car or travel with only a few others – choose cars with a variety of different people in them.
- Never travel in the same car as anyone who is clearly drunk or who seems abusive or violent.
- If you suspect trouble, get off and change cars at the next stop, choosing carefully where to get on next.
- Never use a laptop computer or reveal the location of your wallet or purse. Always keep your valuables close and out of sight.
- Never wait for a train in a unpopulated part of the platform; wait close to others, keeping your valuables from view.
- Avoid making eye contact or conversation with other passengers. Avoid asking for travel directions or looking as though you are lost.
- Never use, get out, or check messages on your cellular phone on a subway.

identification or your destination. Stay as close as you can to an exit, remain alert, and avoid conversation or interaction.

Remain polite

Avoid leaning into other people's space, or, if you have to do so, defuse potential aggression by apologizing or some other conflict-reducing gesture. If you have difficulty breathing, loosen your clothing and try to stand near to an open window. Never push or shove on a crowded train as this could lead to conflict.

Surviving train accidents

Owing to the high speeds at which trains can travel and the fact that most accidents occur either because of impact with another train or a derailment, train accidents usually entail some fatalities when passengers are violently thrown and carriages roll over and crumple. The chances of your survival without injury in such a crash are relatively small, but you can marginally attempt to ready yourself for a crash with enough warning. Signs of derailment include sudden braking, rocking, and cars rolling onto their sides. You should expect to be pitched suddenly across the train. Pulling a coat over your head and your upper body may protect against flying glass and objects.

Remain in the car if possible

After the accident, if you are unable to open a door, pulling off the rubber gaskets on the windows and climbing out, feet first, may be possible. But you should be mindful at all times that laceration by broken glass can be extremely dangerous.

Even if you are unhurt and your car seems stable and unlikely to tip or roll, you may nevertheless be safer remaining within the carriage and waiting for help because the track may be electrified. As soon as you move you risk more injury from broken glass, falling from the car, or giving yourself an electric shock.

What to do if the train is on fire

Fuel spillage can cause fires on trains after a derailment. Should you see flames or smell burning, try to get as far away from the train as possible. If you are trapped in the train, DO NOT open any inner doors, which could cause a rush of air and the fire suddenly to spread. Slam shut all the doors and use luggage to break open a window, escaping if you can jump from the carriage without injury. Tightly wrap a coat or travel blanket around yourself for protection against the glass. Be aware that the tracks may be electrified and that fuel spilled outside of the train may also present a fire hazard.

In a train crash

If you survive a train accident, do not leave the carriage unless you are certain that there is no danger of being electrocuted on the line below. It is probably safer to remain inside the carriage, where you are probably less likely to incur further injury.

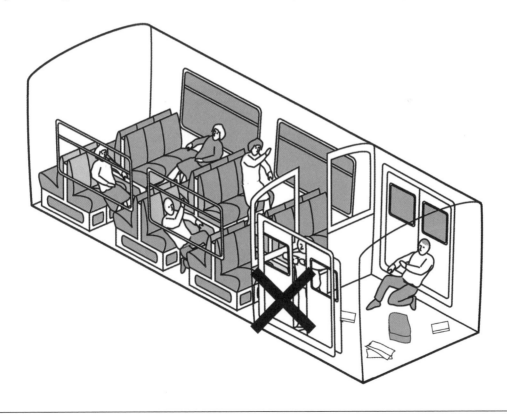

AIRCRAFT SAFETY

Flying can be a stressful and uncomfortable experience. Long-haul flights can be particularly hazardous to the health because sitting for long periods of time in cramped conditions can cause serious circulation problems. Developing deep vein thrombosis when flying has been widely publicized in recent years, owing to the deaths of even relatively young passengers on longer haul and sometimes even short-haul flights.

A risk to consider

Deep vein thrombosis occurs when blood clots in the deep veins of the legs. A clot that passes up the blood vessels and through the heart can become lodged in one of the small blood vessels supplying the lungs. The result is that the oxygen supply to the body can be cut off, a condition known as pulmonary embolism. Warning signs of this condition are reduced blood flow, chest pain, and shortness of breath, all of which may result in lung damage and possibly even death.

Who is at risk?

Certain people are more at risk than others when flying. These include pregnant women, women taking the contraceptive pill, or people who have had a recent operation, are aged over 40, or who have cardiovascular disease (for example, high blood pressure, high cholesterol, or a previous stroke). For these people in particular, the slowing of blood flow from the legs back to the heart as they sit for long periods in the aircraft increases the danger of blood clots. People who have had recent surgery or varicose veins removed are also more susceptible, as is anyone who has suffered from heart failure, cancer, obesity, or blood-clotting problems. However, it is important to remember that, in general, deep vein thrombosis affects men and women equally and can occur in all different adult age groups.

Staying healthy during a flight

Restricted legroom can make this slowed blood flow even more dangerous, especially if the back of the seat in front is pressing on

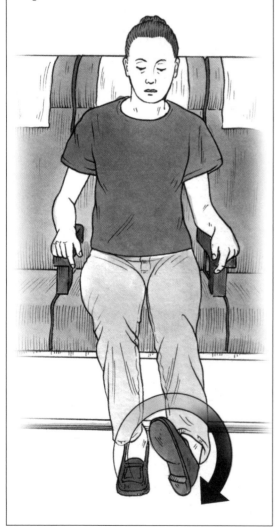

Preventing deep vein thrombosis

Rotating your ankles, clenching and unclenching leg muscles, and raising your legs during your flight will help to prevent deep vein thrombosis.

Avoiding deep vein thrombosis

- Drink plenty of water, and avoid alcoholic drinks and caffeine – dehydration increases the risk.
- Never remain in your seat throughout the flight, walk around the plane regularly, at least every hour.
- Avoid crossing your legs, or sitting in the same position for a prolonged period.
- Wear loose comfortable clothing and keep your leg area free.
- While seated, lift your legs and flex the calf muscles every half hour, rotating the ankles for a few minutes each time.
- Never spend the entire flight asleep and never take sleeping pills that could keep you motionless for hours.
- Taking an aspirin one hour before flying is not a guaranteed prevention but can make it more difficult for blood to clot.
- Wearing support stockings when flying can help to massage the legs and increase circulation.

the front of the legs. Even passengers in first and business class can suffer blood clots in their legs – extensive legroom is not necessarily a sure means of avoiding blood clots. The key to preventing deep vein thrombosis is to move regularly and clench the lower limbs, in order to create muscle contractions that keep the deep vein blood flowing back to the heart by compressing the veins' walls. Simply exercising your muscles during a flight greatly reduces your chances of becoming ill as a result of a circulatory disorder.

Some airlines provide instructions on how to exercise your legs, but simply rotating your ankles, clasping a pillow between your calves and raising your legs, tightening and relaxing the leg muscles and getting up and moving around the plane at frequent intervals, all help to prevent deep vein thrombosis. You should also be able to recognize the signs of deep vein thrombosis and, if on getting off the plane you have extreme swelling or pain in your legs, you should contact a doctor immediately.

Jet lag and high blood pressure

Other health problems when travelling by plane are far less serious. Jet lag can be unpleasant, but can be avoided if you can get your body in sync with local daylight hours.

Taking melatonin, a natural hormone produced by the pineal gland, can work for jet lag and its resulting insomnia. Psychological problems associated with flying, for example, fear of flying and claustrophobia, can lead to physical health problems, such as high blood pressure and migraines. Consulting with your doctor before you fly may be helpful in reducing stress levels.

Avoid alcohol, drink water

Dehydration is an inevitable consequence of flying caused by the dry stale air in the cabin. Drinking large amounts of water, before, during and after flying, and avoiding alcohol and caffeine help to reduce dehydration. Intestinal gas is another common complaint because, as the plane ascends and the pressure in the cabin falls, the volume of trapped gases rises, making us feel bloated. Drinking large amounts of water and avoiding leafy vegetables helps to prevent gas. Drink water at regular intervals, and take an extra bottle onto the plane with you. Never rely on the airline's service for your water intake, as it is usually inadequate. Anyone who has had recent abdominal, eye, chest, or central nervous system surgery should avoid flying altogether as gas build-ups could pose a serious health risk.

Positions to avoid

However brief the flight, never remain seated with your legs crossed throughout. Get up and walk around, clench and unclench leg muscles, and keep your legs uncrossed.

General flying health tips

- Use saline nose drops or nasal saline spray to keep your nasal passages lubricated, reducing reduce the risk of airborne infection.
- Never wear contact lenses on any flight lasting longer than 4 hours – dry lenses and dry eyes can result in corneal damage.
- Avoid flying if you are ill or recuperating.
- Feet tend to swell when

flying – wear comfortable shoes and rotate your ankles often.
- Using an eye mask, earplugs, neck rest, and blow-up pillow can improve the quality of your sleep for short periods.
- Always report to the cabin crew if the aircraft is stuffy because, on some aircraft, the air flow can usually be adjusted.

Take precautions to alleviate mild symptoms

In general, when flying, medication should be kept close at hand. If you are asthmatic or subject to severe allergic reaction, be sure to fly with your medication in your carry-on bag. If you are allergic, avoid eating airline snacks that may contain traces of nuts. Pack decongestant medication to avoid ear and sinus discomfort caused by cabin pressure. Chewing gum to alleviate ear pain during take-off and landing, and using a nasal spray can help you to avoid nasal pain.

Keeping nasal passages moist using a spray or natural oils will help to protect you from infection from airborne illnesses transmitted in the recycled stale air of the cabin. Carrying extra supplies of bottled water on board is a wise measure. You can protect your skin from the effects of dry air by using moisturizing lotion and lip balm.

COPING WITH AIR RAGE PASSENGERS

Since the events of 11 September 2001, stringent security checks are in place around the world. However, an air travel hazard similar to the terrorist threat yet much harder to prevent is the air rager, whose tendencies may ironically be triggered by the new increased security measures. One cause of air rage is alcohol – a passenger who drinks heavily before and during the flight may become violent. Another cause of air rage is mental instability, a much more difficult condition to detect.

Check out your fellow passengers

The first rule when waiting to board the plane is to remain alert and watchful, and to observe your fellow passengers. Many passengers betray signs that give some warning of their behaviour, even while they are still on the ground. If a passenger appears drunk or unruly, or is acting suspiciously, however small or strange – you should notify the airline staff immediately and make it clear that you do not wish to travel on the same plane as the individual.

Once you are on board the plane, maintain such vigilance and take note of all those around you and of the safety exits. If another passenger is acting strangely, or violently, avoid confrontation and notify the flight crew, obeying all their instructions as they come to assist you.

Let the flight crew take charge

Never attempt to take the situation into your own hands: air flight crew are extensively trained and will know how to handle the situation. Delegating to them is wisest, unless they themselves appear to lose control of the situation, for example, if the unruly passenger overpowers them and escapes.

Generally airline staff will first of all attempt to defuse the situation and appease the passenger who is causing disruption. They may seem to indulge the passenger or make unrealistic promises: do not object to any of their suggestions, as often such appeasements are made in the interests of safety and as a means of managing a dangerous situation. Never stare at the disruptive person

because it could trigger even worse behaviour. If you are seated next to them or nearby, ask to be moved if possible, and distance yourself, avoiding eye contact.

Be prepared to help out

A more serious scenario will involve the air rager losing all inhibitions and acting out

Check exits

Once you have boarded the plane, make a note of the nearest exit in case you need to use it in an emergency.

suddenly and unpredictably. These instances are extremely rare, but there have been cases of passengers attempting to open doors in midair, to kick out windows, and even assaulting pilots. In such situations, you will need to act fast to support the crew. For this reason, never ignore commotion in the cabin, but be prepared to take some action.

Try to remain calm and in control of yourself, and avoid taking the situation personally if the air rager insults or threatens you. Keep your mind focused on the safety risks at stake and on how you can best assist airline staff. If you find yourself helping to restrain the threatening passenger, be mindful of their nose and mouth, and keep air passages free in order to avoid suffocating them. Air crews may use handcuffs, rope, or cargo straps when dealing with disruptive passengers, but you may be forced to tie hands with the sleeves of sweaters or other materials close at hand.

SAFETY MEASURES DURING EXTREME TURBULENCE

Turbulence can be hard to predict and usually occurs without warning. It is created by a number of different conditions, including atmospheric pressures, jet streams, cold or warm fronts, or thunderstorms. Although pilots fly planes to avoid storm systems, hitting what are known as 'air pockets' is a common cause of turbulence and cannot be altogether avoided. In most cases, the effect is mild bumping of the plane, rather like a boat on choppy water. However, extreme turbulence, while highly unlikely to cause damage to the plane's robust structure, can throw passengers and staff about the plane, causing injury and sometimes even death.

Among non-fatal accidents, in-flight turbulence is the leading cause of injuries to airline passengers and flight attendants, and incidents are higher among those not wearing seat belts.

In order to be prepared, it is necessary to first understand the different kinds of turbulence that may be encountered. Panicking during light turbulence causes undue stress, and all passengers should learn to anticipate a little light turbulence and to endure short periods of discomfort without irrational fear of injury. Most turbulence is harmless.

Light turbulence
- Slight strain against seat belts and shoulder straps
- Little or no difficulty experienced walking about the cabin
- Erratic changes in movement

Moderate turbulence
- Changes in aircraft altitude and attitude
- Stronger strain against seat belts
- Unsecured objects dislodged
- Difficulty walking through the cabin

Severe turbulence
- Major abrupt changes in the aircraft's attitude
- Occupants forced violently against seat belts
- Unsecured objects lifted from the floor
- Walking through the cabin impossible

Turbulence can occur with almost no warning, so it is therefore recommended that passengers remain seated with their seat belts on at all times – except when moving

Warning signs of air rage

- **Under influence of alcohol or drugs**
- **Bizarre or strange manner**
- **Disorderly loud groups**
- **Loud, abusive language**
- **Arguments or possible domestic conflict between couples or families**

Turbulence

In air journeys, turbulence caused by poor weather conditions is nearly always inevitable. The aircraft pilot will usually inform passengers well ahead of time for any turbulence that may occur, and the seatbelt sign will light up and should be adhered to.

about to exercise calf muscles. As soon as light turbulence is experienced, airline staff will advise you to return to your seat and fasten your seat belt. During extreme turbulence, however, airline staff will be seated themselves, and they may not always be in a position to reassure or offer guidance.

Remain calm and belted up

At this point, you will need to remain calm and sit as tight as possible. Although baggage is usually secured in overhead compartments, there is a danger of it falling and being thrown around the plane; however, a more serious danger is striking your head against the roof of the plane as it drops and ascends violently. Remaining in your seat with the seat belt tightly fastened is absolutely essential. Most fatalities that have occurred during extreme turbulence on major air carriers were among those not wearing their seat belt. Similarly, the majority of serious injuries resulting were also among those not wearing their seat belts.

CHAPTER SIX

Terrorist threats

Despite the attack on the World Trade Center in New York City on 11 September 2001, since the 1980s terrorist activity has actually declined worldwide.

The heyday of global terrorism was the 1970s and 1980s. By the mid-1980s, more than 800 international terrorist organizations were in operation. In 1986 alone, these organizations were responsible for 897 incidents, the high point of terrorist activity. Since then, terrorist activity has been contracting. In 1987, the figure fell to 666 incidents; in 1993, 427. By 1994, there were only 321 terrorist attacks globally, and the figures have steadied around this mark to date (data: US State Department).

Counterbalancing these figures is the fact that fatalities and injuries from terrorist attacks have increased since the 1970s. While in the 1970s property attracted 70 per cent of terrorist assaults and people 30 per cent, the equation has now reversed. Death tolls now have more currency for terrorists than shattered structures. This, combined with the fact that increasingly lethal weapons technologies are available illegally, means there is no room for complacency.

The threat of terrorism varies considerably with international location. The United States still remains one of the places least likely to suffer terrorist outrage in crude numbers of incidents. Israel, by contrast, is currently experiencing bombings at a rate of one or two a week, with enormous impact on the social and cultural life of the nation. Yet the lesson of 11 September is a cautionary one. Wherever we live, we can no longer ensure immunity from terrorism.

HOW TERRORISTS SELECT TARGETS

Terrorist actions usually have two objectives. First, to raise the political profile of their cause, expediting their agenda with relevant governments. Secondly, to remove facilities or people directly or indirectly opposed to their cause. These two objectives affect the most important element of a terrorist outrage – target selection.

Simply living in an urban environment makes you a possible target for terrorism. Terrorism is an overwhelmingly urban phenomenon. Towns and cities provide the terrorist with anonymity, a proximity to centres of influence and research (such as government buildings) and easy access to logistics and supplies. More significantly, they also present a high density of targets in a limited area.

Terrorist targets in urban areas fall into several categories. Their selection is usually dictated by the resources and levels of expertise available to the terrorist group.

Public places

Often selected for indiscriminate bomb attacks, the most common public targets are those with heavy civilian traffic – nightclubs, bars, restaurants, shopping malls and centres, busy streets, and tourist attractions. Places often frequented by government or military personnel are specifically targeted.

Significant buildings

Buildings are targeted that: 1) represent the values to which the terrorist is opposed; 2) conduct business affecting his interests; and 3) are crucial to the function of the target society. Government and military buildings are a natural choice, as are those with infra-structural importance, such as power plants, nuclear facilities, or chemical works. Places that represent ideological, educational, or religious values are also vulnerable, including churches and mosques, universities, and major libraries.

Aircraft

Planes are exposed to two sorts of terrorist attack: hijacking and bombing. Modern airliners move internationally, so terrorists have many points of entry or access to the aircraft. Standards of airport security vary according to country. Terrorists can select an airport according to their capabilities and their funds for getting there.

Airports are places where an intense mix of foreign faces is present, ensuring visual anonymity for the terrorist. Airlines operating to or within the Middle East or the former Soviet republics are particularly prone to terrorist incidents.

Public vehicles

European and Middle Eastern terrorism has frequently targeted cars and public transport. Such targets ensure significant public disruption. Generally, bombs either planted on board the vehicle or detonated in proximity assault such targets. Train hijackings are far rarer. The large size of a train and its easy access when stationary make it a difficult target for terrorists to secure.

Individuals

Deliberate selection of random, individual civilians is rare. More likely to be targeted are the following:

- Government officials, particularly those with a key role in relation to foreign policy or, by contrast, local government officials who are easily accessible.
- Significant business leaders. Those with international trade links or who handle government contracts tend to be more vulnerable.
- Journalists and publishers, especially working in fields of political analysis or foreign reporting.
- Political activists. Those who are directly or indirectly opposed to the politics or cause of the terrorist organization.

- Significant workers. Workers in important enterprises – such as nuclear power station workers – may be targeted as a group.
- The families of all the above.

The list of targets presented above is not exhaustive. Indeed, one of the terrorists' main strengths is their unpredictability. They can select targets according to simple vulnerability, rather than status.

BOMB HOAXES

Traditionally, terrorists have attacked their targets using four main methods: hoax, bombings, shootings, hostage taking. The bomb hoax is the most inexpensive and low-risk of all terrorist activity, but one capable of major disruption. For the cost of nothing more than a phone call, terrorists can achieve the evacuation of an entire city block, mobilization of emergency services and even military units, widespread disruption to business and traffic, and a general anxiety among the population.

TERRORIST BOMBING

Next comes actual bombings, by far the most popular terrorist tactic. Bombs are delivered in different forms, including booby traps, satchel charges, letter bombs, car bombs, remote-controlled

Hostage taking

Rescue options are limited when a hostage is held like this. Negotiation is the usual course of action. Particularly talented snipers can negate the hostage-taker with a head shot, aiming through to the base of the brain. A bullet to this area – known as the medulla oblongata – instantly severs nerve impulses to the limbs, thus stopping the terrorist pulling the trigger as a final death act.

bombs, and suicide bombs. Bombings tend to have two contrasting uses. First, they are applied to create indiscriminate destruction in public places. Secondly, they are used to kill isolated individuals or groups, the excessive force employed being more of a guarantee of success.

ATTACKS BY SHOOTING

Shootings are rarely used outside of developing countries by trained terrorist organizations. A shooting requires close proximity to the target, unless sniping is an option. Fanatical individuals have opened fire on massed crowds, but terrorists usually target single VIPs. Ironically, these individuals are likely to have the heaviest personal security. Bodyguards are trained to spot and handle gunmen, so VIPs are seldom assassinated by this method (the same is not true of bombings).

HOSTAGE-TAKING

In terms of hostage taking, journalists, businessmen, embassy staff, and government officials working abroad are the most exposed. Countries in states of war, revolution, or civil unrest offer the best conditions for hostage taking and indeed for most kinds of terrorist activity. Turbulent nations seldom have the security services or even political will to deal with a hostage situation, while the terrorists often enjoy the protection of local warlords or captured territories.

Follow official advice when abroad

If abroad, do not flout government advice to leave a country. Follow the lead of your embassy staff – if they are heading home, then all practical diplomatic ties with your homeland are being severed and any rights to protection will possibly dissolve. Stick near protected compounds, and do not travel without good cause. The dangers of foreign travel are dependent upon the destination. Most governments have foreign offices able to give travel advice on specific destinations and warnings of any dangers.

THREAT RESPONSE

If you seriously identify yourself as a possible target both in terms of your individual status and the places you frequent, you have several courses of action. First, ensure that there is security at work. Choose (or lobby for) a reputable security company with a good client portfolio. Having ex-military (particularly special forces) soldiers on their staff is an advantage. They have been trained for the full spectrum of threat assessment and response, and have the training to be of genuine worth in a crisis.

Check references thoroughly

Any non-military staff should show evidence of professional training and accreditation. View the company's training program for staff. It should be comprehensive and include elements such as bomb-threat awareness, surveillance, location security, and even close-protection services. Having a personal bodyguard is the ultimate in anti-terrorist protection, but few have the money or the actual reason to employ such a person.

If you do, make sure that you pay for a highly trained individual. Check his or her references diligently. If he claims to be ex-military, find out his unit, number, and years of service, and approach either the military unit or a regimental association for verification. If he is civilian-trained, check out his training centre and programme.

Be particularly wary of training schools that promise permanent employability in their publicity. No school can make that sort of promise before meeting the candidate, and their training is unlikely to be of quality unless they are of truly international repute.

Avoid a regular routine

Travel presents the greatest opportunities for terrorist attack. Vary your everyday routes to work, and alter the times and method of travel. Terrorist planning often hinges on routine. Choreographing a hijacking or the detonation of a bomb relies on a timetable and the expectation of the target being in a certain place at a certain time. Targets are held under surveillance for some time to ascertain their movements prior to an attack. If those movements are unpredictable or erratic, then the target opportunities are dramatically decreased. Particularly important individuals should also see that their families to obey this rule.

Plan routes defensively

Routes of travel all contain vulnerable points – places ideal for an attack. Usually these are points at which a vehicle must come to a halt, such as traffic lights, junctions, and roundabouts, or concealed places, including tunnels, roads passing through thick woodland, or down narrow alleyways. Blind bends, steep gradients, or one-way streets also present opportunities to set up stop points. Basically, routes should be selected with as few stops as possible, using open roads and with the least danger of being held up in heavy traffic.

Only follow these general anti-terrorist measures if you have serious cause to believe that you are a justifiable target. Terrorist organizations thrive on public paranoia, and there is no need to contribute to this unless you sensibly and reasonably perceive a genuine risk. More indiscriminate target selection, however, means you might still be susceptible to terrorist activity, even if just by being in the wrong place at the wrong time.

BOMBS

Unless a warning is given, little preparation is possible for dealing with a terrorist explosion. Most of us do not live in war zones. We do not expect to be caught in a bomb blast in the course of our daily routine. Yet certain precautions are possible

Suspicious package

A package exhibiting the signs of a possible parcel bomb or chemical/biological device, such as oily stains, badly written address, excessive postage, protruding wires, and strange bulges in the contours.

to thwart some of the terrorist's most common methods of explosive deployment.

Make office windows safer

On a general level, if you work in a building which may attract terrorist attention, it pays to implement some simple anti-bomb measures. The intense blast-wave generated by high explosives shatters glass at considerable distance. Closer to the blast, the particles of glass will, in effect, become razor-sharp high-velocity projectiles quite capable of inflicting fatal injuries. Special shatterproof film is available to place as a laminate over windows and other glass surfaces. It reduces harmful splintering under impact or pressure.

More expensively, laminated glass can be fitted instead of regular window glass. Also remember to fit protective laminates to glass in internal corridors. Blast waves in buildings use corridors as easy routes of travel and create horrifying destruction. Any destructible fitting will add to the storm of shrapnel.

Mail room security

The security expert Peter Consterdine, in his recommended work *The Modern Bodyguard: The Manual of Close-Protection Training* (Protection Publications, Leeds, 2000), also sensibly advises that mail rooms are not located in the centre of buildings. A blast in the heart of a structure may well bring the whole structure down.

Letter or parcel bombs

Bombs of this type range in size from padded envelopes to large parcels. When evaluating any incoming letter or package, first ask yourself if you are expecting a delivery, particularly one from the country or region indicated by the stamps or postal mark. Large or bulky parcels usually contain goods, and in most cases you will have ordered them. If the parcel is unsolicited or does not correspond with an event such as a birthday (in which case you will probably recognize the handwriting on the address or the place of postage), you should instantly treat it suspiciously.

The next stage is to look at the address. The following are warning signals:

● The name and address are badly typed or written, or contain many spelling mistakes. Such could indicate a foreign author unfamiliar with your language.
● Excessive postage. The sender has not had the parcel weighed and priced at a post office.
● No return address. The sender does not want to be identified.
● Restrictive markings such as 'Personal' or 'Private'. They signal a desire for the letter

Suitcase bomb

A suitcase bomb containing a nuclear weapon will usually have a one kiloton yield – the explosive force of 1000 tons of conventional TNT explosive, enough to kill more than 100,000 people in a densely populated city centre.

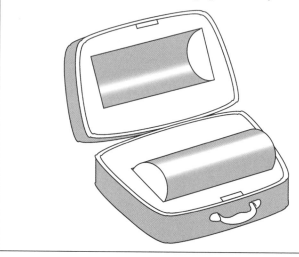

or package to end up in the hands of a specific person without passing through a secretary as intermediary.
● Posting from a foreign country. Identify the country, and note whether there is a particular reason mail should have come from there.

After the mailing information has been assessed, move on to the general shape and appearance of the package:

● Is the package an irregular shape? Bombs are rarely uniformly rectangular.
● Is it of excessive weight for its size, indicating that metal is a key element of the contents?
● Are there any oily stains or strange staining on the packaging? A bomb requires some engineering, and the evidence of this process may be apparent on the outside of the package.

Response to possible anthrax-contaminated letters

- Avoid shaking or emptying the contents of the envelope.
- Avoid passing it around to other members of staff. Make a note of anyone who was in the room when the letter was opened, and hand this list later to the police.
- Do not rub your eyes, nose, or mouth.
- Place in a plastic bag and seal well with tape. If none is available, cover with a cloth and do not touch.
- Turn off air conditioning and fans in the room to prevent the agent circulating in the air.
- Evacuate the room containing the letter. Close the doors and windows, and prevent other people entering the room.
- Wash your hands well, then use the telephone to call the police or emergency authorities.

- Any protruding wires, pieces of metal, or bits of foil visible?
- If you are dealing with a letter, is it unusually rigid?
- Does the package have excessive amounts of packaging material such as masking tape, string, reams of brown paper, and so on? The packaging may be required to contain a heavy explosive device or prevent the contents being revealed prior to delivery. The sender may also feel that the packaging will defeat any bomb-detection technologies.
- Does the package make a sloshing sound when moved? If it does, it could contain a liquid-based explosive.

If a letter or package is considered to be suspicious, do not touch, probe, or shake it. Note that the above signs could also indicate a letter or parcel containing a chemical/biological agent such as anthrax. Treat with added suspicion if there is any powder coming from the package. With all suspect mail, inform the police, and clear people away from the object. Stop other people entering the room after you. Evacuate the building if the bomb threat is acute.

CAR BOMBS

Detecting a car bomb is more difficult than detecting a parcel bomb, as there are generally fewer obvious elements to arouse suspicion. Car bombs vary in their sophistication, placement, and method of detonation, but there are basically two types.

First, there are small devices planted in an inconspicuous part of either the bodywork or the interior. These are usually detonated by remote control, timer, motion switch, pressure switch, tilt device, thermal detonator, barometric detonator, or chemical switch.

Secondly, the entire boot of the car may be filled with explosives to form a massive device. Such huge bombs are generally directed against property, and they will be parked close to the target and detonated by timer or remote control.

Secure your car

If there is a chance you might attract terrorist activity, your car requires dedicated security arrangements. When not in use, keep it in a locked and alarmed garage. Ideally, do not leave it for long periods unguarded by the side of a road or in a public place. Have it serviced only by reputable engineers with good overnight vehicle-security measures. In particularly dangerous foreign countries, do not wash the car if possible. Dirty bodywork shows up evidence of human interference quite conspicuously. Unexplained finger marks around the wheel arches, door sills, and

Complete vehicle search

When conducting a comprehensive vehicle search, take the following steps. Touch the vehicle as little as possible throughout the search.

● *Check from a distance*
First inspect the car from a distance. Walk around the vehicle looking for any obvious signs of disturbance. Pay attention to the ground around the vehicle. Does it show evidence of human activity, such as footprints, jacking indentations, tyre marks, pieces of discarded paper or wire, patches of oil? Can you see anything out of place on the car? Does it appear to have moved slightly from its original position? Is any glass cracked or broken? Are wires or brake cables hanging loose?

● *Is anyone suspicious nearby?*
Anything different from the way the car commonly looks should act as a warning. Also study the surrounding area. Can you see anybody acting suspiciously in the distance, possibly watching you? (They may be waiting to detonate the bomb by remote control.)

● *Check for any scratches and smudges*
Close distance with the car and examine all external surfaces. Are there scratches around the locks? Are their any marks – including fingerprints, scratches, smudges, oil prints, indentations, and staining – on the paintwork, glass, mirrors, plastic parts, or chrome?

● *Is anything different?*
Visually check whether the doors, trunk/boot, or bonnet are part open or if they appear to have been recently forced. Look inside the vehicle. Have seats been moved from their usual position? Are there any wires visible in the seat belt reels? Do some internal switches appear to have been put in the 'on' position? Have floor mats been moved, or are they dirtier than you left them?

● *Check the lower vehicle*
Squat down and look around the wheels, wheel arches, and door sills. Are there any visible devices? Have the wheels been tampered with? Look for evidence such as loosened wheel nuts or objects pushed into tyre tread or walls.

● *Look underneath the car*
Get right down on the floor and scan the entire underneath of the vehicle. Pay special attention to the area around the gas/petrol tank and the exhaust pipe. (A gas tank igniting will do much of the bomb's work, and the exhaust pipe might be used as a heat source for a thermal detonator.)

● *Cautiously check the trunk*
Check the trunk. Open it slowly, scanning for suspicious wiring as its opens. Examine it for devices, using the minimal amount of touch. (This stage should actually be the first time during the search you have had to touch the vehicle at all.) Examine the spare tyre and its recess. Lift up any mats. Check the wall of the trunk around the gas tank for signs of cutting or lifting.

● *Check doors and interior*
Open a car door and inspect the interior. Do this very slowly and carefully, inspecting the hinge in particular for any wires. A plastic strip can be used to probe hidden angles of the door without danger of making an electrical circuit. Open all four doors by this method. Once open, conduct a thorough search of the interior. Check every recess, fitting, and compartment methodically, including ashtrays, audio speaker/player fittings and cup holders.

Priority features for car search

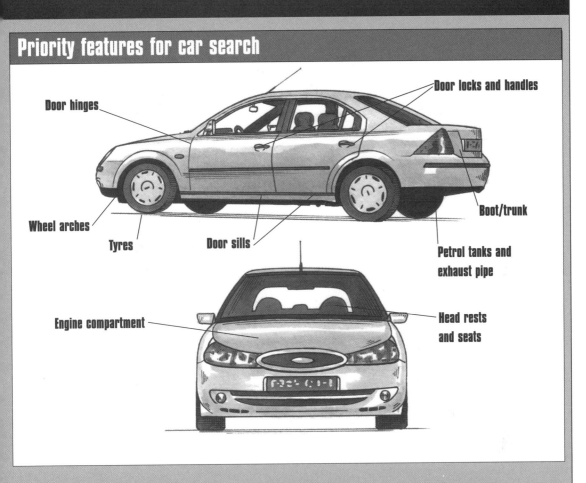

Door hinges

Door locks and handles

Wheel arches

Tyres

Door sills

Boot/trunk

Petrol tanks and exhaust pipe

Engine compartment

Head rests and seats

Through this part of the search, refrain from leaning on seats in case there is a device planted beneath and operated by pressure.

● *Check under the hood*
Release the hood/bonnet. This is best done using two people – one should hold the hood down to stop it springing up when the catch is released. Lift the hood with the same precautions

as opening doors. Once the hood is open, conduct a thorough check. Is there any suspicious wiring going from electrical sources or motors? Confirm that fluid compartments such as washer bottles contain only regular fluid. Have the radiator or oil filler caps been tampered with? This stage assumes a good working knowledge of what your car engine looks like.

● *Switch on and listen*
Finally, enter the car and turn on the engine. Listen for any unusual sounds. When first driving off, are there any unfamiliar sensations in the gears or the driving action?

If any device is discovered, or there are very suspicious disturbances, clear the area of people (including yourself) and contact the police.

EOD vehicle

Explosive ordnance disposal (EOD) vehicles are a remote means of inspecting suspect devices or packages, and destroying them if necessary using an on-board remotely fired rifle.

prevent the easy fitment of such a device. In contrast to the bodywork, keep the vehicle's interior spotlessly clean and tidy to expose any interference there.

How to check for a terrorist device

Practically, however, there is often no way of avoiding leaving your car unattended. You should therefore know the basics of how to conduct a vehicle search. Vehicle searches vary in degree according the reality of the threat and the period for which the vehicle has been left. A brief separation from the vehicle of only a few minutes may require only a simple search of about the same period of time. A prolonged absence in a public place will upgrade the search length to a couple of hours. Again, vehicle searches are only required if you are under genuine terrorist threat. There is little need to follow these procedures unless terrorist intentions have a specific connection with you.

The vehicle arousing suspicion may not be your car at all, but a mobile bomb parked ready for detonation. The following characteristics should arouse your suspicions immediately:

hood/bonnet might suggest the planting of a device. Remember, though, it takes only seconds to place a magnetic bomb under the sill of a car, and there may be no immediate visual evidence of the threat.

One way of counteracting this is to keep the wheel arches and sills heavily greased to

- The vehicle is parked illegally near a significant building or possible target.
- The vehicle is sitting down heavily on its suspension at the rear. Such may indicate

that the trunk/boot contains a heavy explosive device. Many improvised explosives are made from bags of agricultural fertilizer, which have considerable weight.

- You have never seen the vehicle before in that particular area.
- An unknown vehicle is parked along the route or place of a special event – such as a military parade or government ceremony.
- The vehicle appears to have been abandoned.

Your first recourse when dealing with any suspicious vehicle is the police. Try to keep people away from the vehicle, and wait until the police bomb disposal unit arrives. Naturally, you must not let your imagination run away with you. The police will be far from happy if you call them out on such a potentially serious matter for every unfamiliar vehicle that you encounter.

If it is your vehicle you are concerned about, conduct a basic vehicle search. Check the external bodywork for any signs of tampering. Squat down and examine the wheels, wheel arches, and door sills for any planted devices. Look underneath the car and note anything out of the ordinary, particularly around the gas/petrol tank and exhaust pipe. Scan the car interior to see if any seats, floor mats, or switches have been moved. Finally, open the car door slowly, looking for any wires appearing as the door swings open. If wires are spotted, stop opening the door, and move well away from the vehicle.

SUICIDE BOMBS

Bombers who are killed when they detonate their own bomb are not a new or uncommon phenomenon, but their recent usage in terrorist action against Israel has brought them into the headlines. Western governments have raised the spectre of suicide bombings in Europe and the United States as a continuation of the September 11 attacks.

Suicide bombers tend to select public places such as shopping centres and bars as their targets. Some also board packed buses. Their weapon is packs of explosive, usually strapped around the torso and upper thighs. To circumvent security searches, the explosives will sometimes be concentrated in the groin area – police are naturally reluctant to touch this area, particularly if the suicide bomber is a woman. Precautions against suicide bombers are few. They tend to appear quickly and detonate their explosive impulsively. Disguises are used to make them blend in with the crowd. There are a few warning signs available, but there are some basic characteristics of suicide bombers.

What a bomber looks like

Unseasonable clothing is typical sign. Body-carried explosives are bulky, and they require large jackets or overcoats to conceal them. These will be worn even in the height of summer. The clothes may also bulge unnaturally in places. Suicide bombers tend to run their hands nervously over their bodies to make sure that the explosives are in place. The bomber will often stand out as being alone and incongruous. Contrary to the usual assumptions about fanatics, most often appear thoroughly scared at their impending death. They may be perspiring profusely with fear.

Duck and cover

If you suspect an individual, stay well clear, and alert the authorities. Some bombers suddenly declare themselves in the last few moments, exposing the explosives and making an impassioned final statement. Should you ever experience this moment, follow the 'duck and cover' principle used to protect against any source of bomb blast. Throw yourself straight to the floor, and cover your head with your arms. If at all possible, do this behind or beneath some protective object or surface – a table, wall, car, and so on.

Do not try to tackle the suicide bomber or reason with him. In his state of heightened emotion, he is unlikely to retreat from his intended course of action.

BOMBS IN PUBLIC PLACES

In an urban landscape, everywhere from litter bins to toilet cisterns has been used to hide terrorist devices. Here are a few red lights that may lead you to contact the relevant authorities:

- Unattended bags, suitcases, sealed boxes, or other containers placed in public places. Your suspicions should be doubled if you see someone deposit the bag, then walk away. If you are unsure what is happening, tell the person that they have forgotten his or her bag – do not take the bag over to him. His response may tell you something of the container's contents.
- Someone gently depositing a suspicious object into a public waste bin. They may well be looking nervously around to see if they are being watched (note, however, they may simply be illegally dumping household waste).
- Engineers doing unrequested work. If the work is being carried out in your office or neighbourhood, check with local utility companies to see if they have a record of the job. Do the engineers have a dedicated vehicle with an official company name/address/telephone number on the side, or are they using an unmarked private vehicle?

WEAPONS OF MASS DESTRUCTION

Talk of weapons of mass destruction (WMD) in a terrorist context has gained additional currency in the aftermath of the World Trade Center attacks. A series of anthrax biological attacks within the United States and evidence that terrorist organisations have attempted to manufacture nuclear or radio-logical bombs have startled Western governments. Importantly, the risks of

terrorists actually making effective WMDs and successfully deploying them are slight.

WMDs require considerable money, technical and scientific expertise, and supply contacts to produce. Such resources are well beyond most terrorist organisations. That said, the anthrax attacks in the United States demonstrate that threats should be taken seriously, and we should understand some of the procedures for surviving a WMD strike.

BIOLOGICAL/CHEMICAL ATTACK

Letters containing anthrax spores were delivered to several offices and government buildings following the September 11 attacks, resulting in a small number of deaths. Although the fear of chemical/biological weapons is perhaps out of all proportion to the reality of the threat, governments have already taken steps towards emergency preparedness in case of a mass assault on a wide population.

Biological weapons

Anthrax is only one of a vast list of chemical/biological substances that could be used as terrorist weapons. Biological weapons are naturally occurring or artificially cultivated diseases. At the most serious end of the scale they include anthrax, botulism, plague, smallpox, tularaemia, and viral haemorrhagic fevers. All of these, if left untreated, will result in a high percentage of fatalities, in some cases approaching 100 per cent.

Chemical weapons

These agents are manufactured substances designed to assault certain physiological functions. Being specifically designed as weapons often means their lethality is extreme. Such is particularly the case with nerve agents such as Sarin and VX. These instantly attack the victim's central nervous system, and death can result in minutes. As a general rule, the symptoms of chemical agents emerge within minutes and hours, whereas biological agents can take days to produce effects.

Listing the individual agents, their symptoms, and treatments would require a book in itself. For those requiring detailed information, possibly the best source is the Center for Disease Control in Atlanta, Georgia, in the United States. Its website is a major resource for information on chemical/ biological risks, prevention, and treatment. For the purposes of this book, however, we will assess general response measures common to most agent threats as issued by the US Department of State.

External signs

Noticing the presence of a chemical/biological attack may not be easy. Many agents have no sensory presence, and the early symptoms can be confused with common illnesses. There can be, however, some cautionary external signs:

- Visible clouds of dust, vapour, or fog-like moisture, usually low-lying (most agents are heavier than air), sometimes coloured, and generally not related to prevailing climatic conditions.
- Strange smells in the air, especially the scents of almonds, cut grass or hay, or peaches.
- Signs of developing illness in people, particularly respiratory troubles, deterioration in mental condition, sickness, convulsions, strange rashes, and problems with eyesight.
- Dead or dying animals. Fish, in particular, are sensitive to many chemical agents.

How to respond

If these signs correspond with a general chemical/biological alert in the media and the presence of government officials in protective clothing (checking first that they are not on a training exercise), then you should assume the worst.

Your response to a chemical or biological attack should be as follows: 1) try to avoid any possible contamination by the agent; and 2) improvise decontamination.

Stun grenade

The stun grenade is a typical device used in hostage-rescue missions. It produces a blinding flash and excruciating bang which incapacitate but do not injure those in the vicinity.

- Most agents work through inhalation, so simply covering the mouth with a handkerchief or other cloth will provide protection (the ideal is a purpose-designed face mask). Soak the cloth, if possible, in water containing one tablespoon of baking soda.
- Cover any exposed skin with clothing, particularly if it has cuts or abrasions.
- Try to keep upwind of the attack area, and move inside as soon as possible.
- Because of the agent's heavier-than-air properties, move to a high floor in the building.
- Shut and seal all external doors and windows.
- Switch off air conditioning and heating systems, and plug up ventilation holes or any external wall apertures.
- If you are outside in a car, close the air vents and shut the windows tightly.
- Urgently seek medical treatment.

Any suspicion of contact with a chemical or biological agent requires treatment by emergency services. Most developed countries have mobile decontamination and treatment centres for these incidents. Try to follow guidelines issued through reliable media and get to medical treatment as soon as possible. Vaccines can counteract even some of the most virulent agents if they are treated in the early hours of contamination.

How to decontaminate yourself

There are some personal decontamination procedures you can follow in the interim. If you have come in from the outside, try to dispose of your clothing in sealed plastic bags as soon as possible.

Scrub the skin with warm, soapy water. For added strength, add one part bleach to ten parts water.

A dry decontamination option is to cover the skin thickly with talcum powder or flour. Leave it on the skin for about 30 seconds, then brush off with a rag, preferably while wearing rubber gloves. Remember, the powder you brush off may be contaminated, so do not breathe its dust, and isolate yourself from the decontamination room after completion. Cleaning the skin in either of these ways can prevent the agent's absorption into the body.

Safe room for biological/chemical attack

If there is a serious chance of major biological or chemical attack, preparing a safe room in the home or office is an advanced precaution:

- Select a large room on the upper floors of the building. It should have the fewest windows and doors, and preferably access to a bathroom and toilet.
- Close windows and doors, and seal around the edges with adhesive tape. Also plug up any vents, cracks in walls, or gaps in external woodwork.
- Cover windows with plastic sheeting, and tape into place.
- Shut off air conditioning units.
- Stock the room with the following: protective clothing (including rubber gloves and boots, waterproof clothing, face masks, and industrial safety overalls); enough food and water to last three days; first-aid kit and any prescription medicines taken by family members; warm bedding; television set and radio (preferably battery-operated or wind-up) for monitoring the media; fire extinguisher; bottle opener; torch; battery-powered CB radio.

Such measures can help you avoid the worst effects of a chemical-biological attack. There is another threat emerging within the terrorist context, which incites equal fear – radiological, or nuclear attack.

RADIOLOGICAL AND NUCLEAR THREATS

Unlike chemical/biological outrages, nuclear or radiological terrorism has never been witnessed. Yet this does not preclude its use in the future. Poorly controlled stocks of weapons-grade uranium and plutonium in the former Soviet republics are said to be for sale on the worldwide market. The technology for manufacturing a simple suitcase-housed nuclear bomb is comparatively straightforward once you have this material. Such a device would produce an explosive force equivalent to several kilotons of TNT, enough force to devastate a city centre.

'DIRTY BOMBS'

Currently the greatest threat is not, however, explosive devices, but crude radiological weapons popularly termed 'dirty bombs'. These devices consist of a core of conventional high explosive surrounded by pellets of non-weapons-grade radioactive material, usually with low-level radioactivity. The theory behind such weapons is that the conventional explosives are detonated, blasting the radioactive material over a wide area and leading to destructive irradiation of people and property.

Dirty bombs, like so many terrorist WMDs, pose a limited but genuine threat. Because highly radioactive materials is almost always held in secure installations, terrorists would have to resort to low-level elements used in industry or medicine. These have little capability for producing serious illness, but still deserve treating with respect.

How to protect yourself

A dirty bomb detonates just like a conventional bomb, with a localized explosion. The radioactive material is scattered over a range according to the force of the blast, usually several hundred metres maximum, and the collateral dust and debris will also be irradiated. Your first response should be to get away from the explosion site. Avoid the public transport system if at all possible, as you may take radioactive materials into confined public spaces and transport it further afield. Get inside a building and stay inside. Seal doors and windows. Take off your clothes and place them in a sealed garbage bag. Keep these clothes for later professional analysis. Taking a shower will help remove any contamination from the skin, and emergency response services may well deploy portable showers and decontamination units for this purpose.

Do not pick up anything from the scene of the blast, and do not go back to collect personal effects. In particular, do not eat food or drink fluids that have been exposed to the dust of the blast. Some sources recommend taking potassium iodide (KI) to protect the thyroid gland from absorbing any radio-activity. This advice is of limited use. Potassium iodide is only protective against radioactive iodine, and in most cases this will not have been used in the bomb. Also, KI only works if taken prior to exposure. Factor in the dangers of KI to certain individuals and it should be left alone. Always follow the advice of the disaster-response teams and public broadcasts on quality news channels.

NUCLEAR BOMB

The threat from dirty bombs is a realistic one, while that from actual terrorist nuclear explosions is minimal. The chances of surviving a nuclear blast depend on where you are. At ground zero – the epicentre of the blast – a nuclear weapon will generate temperatures of millions of degrees centigrade, blast waves travelling at 6437km/h (4000mph), and a fireball towering miles into the atmosphere. Terrorist planting of a nuclear device would almost certainly be around central governmental and commercial districts of a major city. The further you are from this point of impact, the better your chances of surviving.

The blast

A nuclear explosion follows a set pattern. First, there is a blinding (often literally) flash of white light brighter than the sun. Secondly, an enormous blast wave rushes out from the explosion, causing vast destruction and carrying with it incinerating heat capable of boiling rivers dry in seconds. Thirdly, as the fireball rises into the atmosphere, air is sucked back to fuel the fire and creates a destructive 'suction blast' travelling in the opposite direction to the initial blast. Finally, after the blast has subsided, solid flakes and particles of highly radioactive dust and debris are sucked up into the fireball (an effect producing the distinctive mushroom cloud of an atomic blast) which fall to earth over a long period – small particles can take months to return to earth. This is known as fallout and has the appearance of flaky ash.

Ways to protect yourself

Against such awesome forces, chances of survival are slim near the centre of the blast. Yet as the explosions at Hiroshima and Nagasaki proved, people can survive such events given a reasonable distance (1.6km (1 mile) at

Disorientation techniques

Blindfolding hostages serves several purposes. First, it prevents the hostage from identifying his captors and the location to which he is taken. Secondly, it makes him more compliant, a lack of vision bringing complete dependency on the hostage taker. Thirdly, it enables hostage takers to have better control of groups of hostages.

Vehicle hostage rescue

The vehicle in the centre containing terrorists and hostages is immobilized by a four-point assault (A, B, C, and D) from counterterrorist forces. Working in cooperation, the rescue units will sometimes smash the window glass with special bars before tackling the terrorists. Firing through the glass may result in bullets deflecting into the hostages, although high-velocity weapons can overcome this problem.

minimum) from the epicentre. Response to a nuclear explosion takes the following steps:

1 There is a time lag of a couple of seconds between the flash and the blast wave. Throw yourself flat to the ground, preferably behind a sturdy physical structure or, even better, in a ditch or depression. Cover your head with your hands, and shield your eyes from the blast.

2 Remain on the floor for at least two minutes. This gives adequate time for blasts and counterblasts to pass over you and helps you avoid the many missiles hurtling through the air.

3 Once the blast sequence has passed, get up and move inside as quickly as possible. Look for a stable structure to provide you with shelter from fire, heat, and soon-to-

arrive radioactive fallout. Note: if you are some miles from the blast zone, you may have a period of grace of several hours before the fallout reaches ground level.

4 If you are outside when the fallout begins to drop, cover your mouth with a cloth – avoid inhaling the dust at all costs. Again, your priority is to find a shelter.

Enduring a terrorist nuclear blast is a remote possibility. A far more present threat is that of being taken hostage.

HOSTAGE AND HIJACK SITUATIONS

Terrorists take hostages for three main reasons: 1) to extract information from the hostage; 2) to use the hostages as bargaining chips for their political ends; and 3) to extract ransom money. The treatment

Observation during a hostage-taking situation

In a lengthy hostage-taking situation, some hostages may be released as a goodwill gesture. If you are one of them you will be extensively debriefed by hostage-rescue officers and negotiators who will be relying on your observations. A hostage should therefore attempt to identify the following features about their captors:

● What type of weapons are they carrying?

● How many of them are there?

● Are there any clues to their ethnic or religious origin (for example, headdress, language, prayer observances)?

● Have you witnessed them undertaking engineering work to doors or windows? – they may be planting booby traps for hostage-rescue units.

● Where are they deployed, or do they move around in unpredictable patterns?

● What do they look like? Remember key physical characteristics, as the debriefing officers may ask you to identify the captors from photographs of known terrorists.

● What is their emotional state? Agitated, reasonable, aggressive, moderate and so on?

● How do they respond to contact with a hostage negotiator?

hostages receive while in captivity varies wildly. On occasions, hostages and captors have struck up almost friendly relations, whereas in other cases hostages are executed or tortured without hesitation.

What if you are taken hostage?

Being taken hostage is a terrifying experience, one full of subtle and constant risk. The basic principle of hostage survival is that, the longer the hostage situation progresses, the greater the chances of survival. The first few minutes of the situation are the most serious. The terrorists will be extremely agitated and consequently more liable to use violence if challenged. If an instant escape is not possible, comply straight away with terrorist orders.

When part of a large group of hostages – such as in an aircraft hijack situation – make yourself as inconspicuous as possible. Do not make eye contact with the terrorists. Do not try to reason, bribe, argue, or otherwise engage with them, and avoid visible discussion with the other hostages. If possible, remove conspicuous items of clothing, wealth or status.

Do as you are told

Once the drama of the first few minutes has subsided, you need to steel yourself for a long haul. Do not expect early release, but bear in mind that professional hostage-rescue services will be working hard to ensure your safety. Maintain a low-key presence at all times. If your captors do talk to you, reply with short, sensible answers or sentences which resist debate, particularly about issues such as religion and politics.

The terrorists will usually set rules for behaviour, movement, communication, and toilet visits. Obey them to the letter, but be vigilant for any variation in the rules – terrorists generally like the power of their position and may change policies in order to catch people out.

Remain calm and composed

Your bearing during the hostage situation should be strong and dignified. Signs of weakness such as tears, pleading, or trembling are likely to attract contempt rather than pity from your captors. If the situation extends for long periods, you may find more relaxed

Vehicle assault

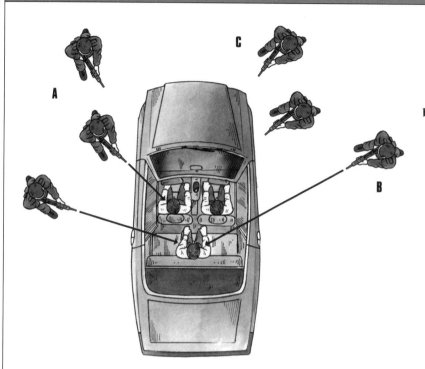

A six-man team makes a vehicle assault to rescue a hostage, here sat in the front right-hand seat. The main body of the assault team (elements A and B) approach from both sides to apprehend the terrorists or, if necessary, eliminate them. Two men (element C) are set aside for the physical rescue.

The same team illustrate a vehicle assault from the rear. Rear assaults are preferable because the terrorists have poorer visual coverage of the situation, and entry into the vehicle is easier because of the direction in which the doors open. If the terrorists have been provided with a car by the security services during a hostage-taking situation, the vehicle will usually have its door locks removed to make future entry easier.

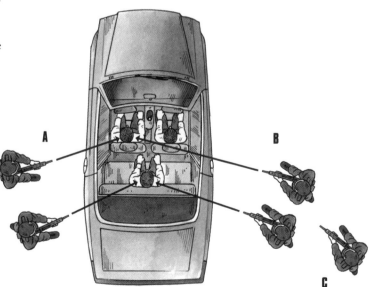

Assault team

A typical police counterterrorist team. The man at the front has a ram-bar to smash down doors, while the remainder of the team carry assorted weapons. The shotgun is primarily used to shoot out door hinges and locks using special blast munitions such as the 'Shok-Lok' or 'Master-Key' rounds.

Emotional response to a hostage situation

Post-release or post-rescue analysis of former hostages has revealed a common sequence of emotional response, depending on how long they were held. The time periods after each category signify the duration of the emotional state.

- Panic and shock (lasting several minutes)
- A sense of disbelief (lasting several hours)
- Heightened anxiety and mounting fear (first hours and days)
- Resistance to or compliance with the hostage situation (can last several weeks or the entire duration of the crisis)
- Depression and demotivation (first weeks to months)

If the captivity lasts beyond a few months, the hostage usually lapses into an acceptance of their situation. They adapt to living under the hostage regime, but may revisit the above categories of response according to particular developments in their situation.

(Source: Department of National Defense, Canada, Peace Support Operations, 2000)

opportunities arise for engaging with the terrorists. Discussions about their cause are fraught with danger, but sometimes unavoidable.

Do not criticize what they are doing, but attempt or appear to understand their point of view. Ask them non-sensitive questions. Do not appear to pry for incriminating information. Should you end up playing card or board games with them, aim to lose as inconspicuously as possible. Be aware of cultural differences. Never assume that the terrorists' culture holds the same values and beliefs as your own.

How to get through captivity

One of the major challenges of surviving a hostage situation is physical and mental discomfort. Hostages are usually kept sitting in confined areas for long periods of time. Boredom and stiff muscles result. To counteract boredom, set your mind logical challenges or explore your memory of personal incidents, films, and books. If you are allowed to read, make sure that what you are reading will not offend your captors. Imagine being in pleasant places to give yourself some mental relief from the surrounding tension, but do not allow yourself to slip away from reality – keep switched on to events around you. Coping with a hostage

Positions of safety

The view a hostage-rescue officer has of an aircraft interior. Hostages should remain firmly in their seats – any sudden movements across the aisle move them into the officer's natural line of fire.

Aircraft hijack survival tips

- Always pay attention to the pre-flight safety briefing so that you know exactly where the emergency doors are. This knowledge could save your life should you have to make an escape.
- Leave your shoes on during a lengthy hostage situation – you do not know when you might have to move quickly.
- Hide any incriminating documents or literature which you may possess.
- If asked for identification, do not show governmental or military papers, only civilian identification.
- Sit in the middle and rear sections of the aircraft if possible. Much terrorist activity will be concentrated around the cockpit at the front of the aircraft.
- When airborne, keep your seat belt fastened.

Room entry

When assaulting a room, hostage-rescue units will first enter with a two-man team – usually preceded by a stun grenade – which separates to opposite corners of the room. The rest of the unit will pour in once the threats are neutralized or to provide back-up against heavy resistance (bottom picture).

Entry method – two man team

Entry method – SWAT unit

situation also demands that you not be self-critical. Realistically, there is little you can do to tackle a motivated and armed terrorist individual. Only if it is evident that the terrorists intend to kill all hostages is violent self-rescue justified.

Accept food and other offers

Keep stretching and tensing limbs, joints, and muscles to maintain blood flow. Use periods in which you are allowed to stand for stretching and exercise. Go to the toilet at every opportunity, and eat and drink when provisions are available.

When rescue arrives

Ironically, one of the most dangerous moments for a hostage is the moment police or military forces attempt a hostage-rescue operation. There may be indicators that such an operation is about to take place. The power to the building, aircraft, or hostage area may be cut suddenly, plunging you into darkness. A loud noise or even explosion outside may be used as a distraction technique to enable hostage-rescue units to deploy.

Hostage-rescue units tend to enter an aircraft or building using stun grenades. These emit a huge bang and a blast of intense light, but cause little physical injury. The assault teams follows closely in the wake of the explosion. Usually they will attempt to neutralize the terrorists with accurate handgun or submachine gun fire, before rather brutally rushing the hostages out to safety. Do not be surprised if once rescued you are hand-cuffed and forced to lie on the floor. This is a common procedure used by rescue units to check whether any terrorists have hidden them-selves among the hostages.

Get down, keep still, and quiet

During a hostage-rescue assault, drop flat on the floor or, if on an aircraft, curl up tightly behind the seat in front of you. The assault units will need clear fields of fire to target the terrorists; standing up could make you an inadvertent target. Keep very still, and do not make any sudden or bold move-ments. Do not shout anything at the rescuers unless critically necessary. All such actions may lead the assault team to class you as a ter-rorist. They are making split-second decisions about who to shoot, and their emotions will be running high.

Finally, comply absolutely with any commands the rescuers make. Reassuringly, most professional hostage-rescue missions result in safe rescue of the majority, if not all, the hostages. This thought should sustain you throughout the crisis.

Autobus hostage rescue

While two soldiers (B) provide cover for the length of the bus, element C performs a seat-by-seat search. One soldier (A) **remains outside the bus to cover the driver's position while another two (D) cover the bus's emergency exits at the rear.**

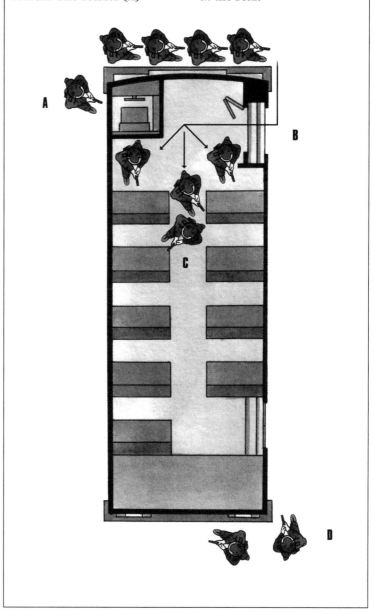

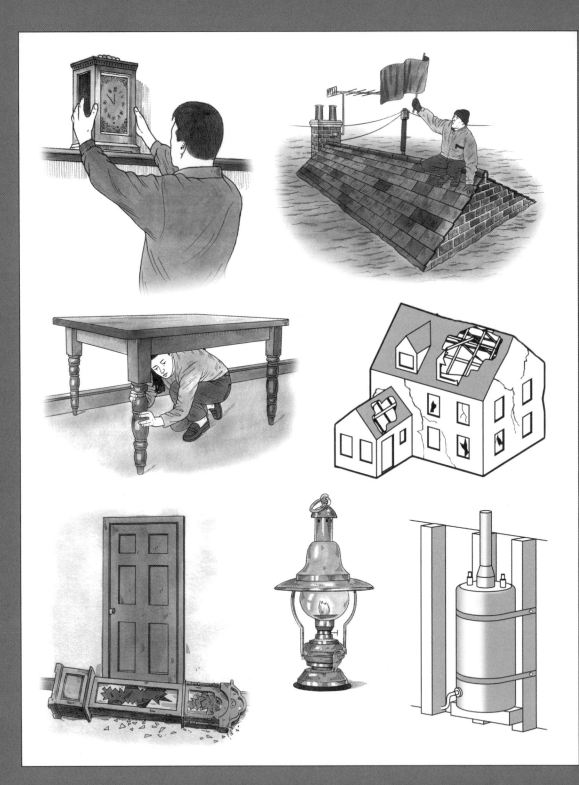

CHAPTER SEVEN

Natural and social disasters

A hurricane, tornado, violent storm, or earthquake is capable of transforming even the most advanced urban location into a chaotic landscape filled with unfamiliar and hidden dangers.

Fast-moving contaminated flood waters, downed electricity lines, snow drifts, and collapsing buildings will confront an often largely completely unprepared public with life-and-death situations. Only by informing yourself in advance, and understanding the complexity of each disaster scenario and its likely impact, do you stand a chance of avoiding the common pitfalls and myths of disaster response. Your preparedness could not only save your life, but also the lives of others.

PREPARING YOUR PROPERTY

Utilities such as electricity, gas, and water are almost always affected by major disasters. Therefore, understanding how to disconnect utilities and the potential hazards associated with your utility connections and appliances is extremely important. Always keep a flashlight near the electricity mains supply, the tool for turning the gas meter close to the gas meter, and a wrench for turning off water by your water supply lever.

Check the location of each utility source in the home, and find out how to turn it off. Water may be turned off at either of two locations: at the main meter, which controls the water flow to the entire property, or at the water main leading into the home.

Secure heavy appliances

Utility connections that are ruptured in a disaster can cause fires, explosions, and floods: for this reason, all appliances should

Prepared for power cuts

Keep a flashlight close to the fuse box at all times. Don't forget to ensure that the batteries remain fresh so that **your flashlight will work if and when you need to resort to it following a power cut or in an emergency.**

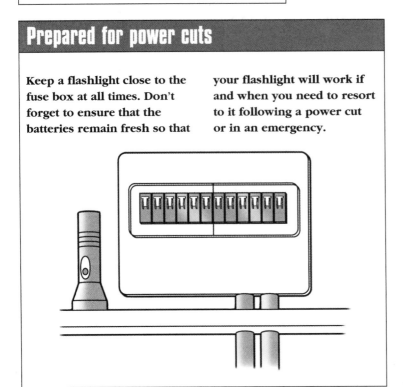

system to deal with flooding. Your home's sewer system should ideally have a back-flow valve because, as flood waters enter the sewer system, sewage can back up and enter your home.

Have a licensed plumber install an interior or exterior backflow valve in accordance with your local building department permit require-ments. Your main electric circuit breaker panel should be at least 30cm (12in) above your local projected flood elevation. Connecting all electrical receptacles in your home to a ground fault interrupter (GFI) circuit will further help to reduce the risk of electrocution. Your washer and dryer, furnace or boiler, and water heater should also all be elevated above potential flood waters on masonry blocks or concrete.

Structural safety

The next consideration is your home's roof and potential structural defects. In a hurricane, tornado, or earthquake, falling tiles and bricks can cause damage and injury: any loose bricks or tiles should therefore be immediately repaired. A badly supported chimney can potentially bring down an entire floor: you may need to consider having the chimney braced by a licensed contractor. Homes with gabled roofs (these look like an A on the ends) are particularly vulnerable to hurricanes and can easily collapse.

In hurricane-prone areas, all homes with a gabled roof should have supportive bracing fitted inside the attic, usually consisting of 50mm x 100mm (2in x 4in) lengths of wood placed in an X pattern from the top centre of the gable to the bottom centre brace of the

be fitted with flexible pipes and secured to walls or to the floor, particularly the heavy water heater, which can cause major damage if it falls through a floor.

If you live in a hurricane or tornado corridor, your home should be secured to its foundations. Many homes built before 1950 lack proper foundation bolts, so it is important that you check this. If your house has wood studs already in place, test the condition of the wood for decay. Consult with a skilled and reliable contractor to ensure that your home is properly fixed to foundation.

Homes prone to flooding

Flooding cannot always be prevented, but knowing the base flood elevation of your home's lowest floor can help you to prepare accordingly. If you live on a flood plain or in a flood-prone area, you should install a floating floor drain plug at the current drain location in your basement, or a sump pump

Securing the water heater

The water heater is very often the heaviest object in the house and can cause major damage or injury if it crashes through floors or falls over. Brace the water heater with metal straps, and mount in a secure unit slightly above floor level. Ensure that flexible pipes and connections that will not rupture in a disaster are used.

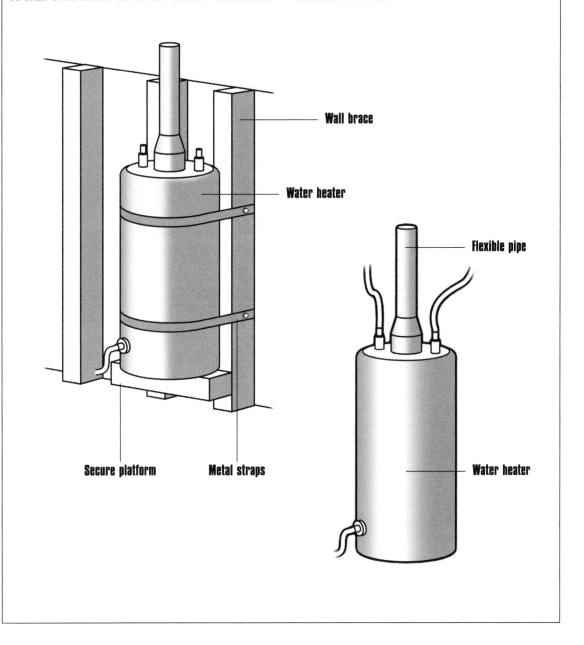

Wall brace

Water heater

Flexible pipe

Secure platform

Metal straps

Water heater

fourth truss, and from the bottom centre of the gable to the top centre brace of the fourth truss. Hurricane straps, designed to help secure any roof by holding it down to the walls, are an excellent addition to any home, if installed by a professional.

Securing doors and windows

It is a commonly held myth that doors and windows should be opened in the event of a hurricane or tornado. Nothing could be further from the truth, and, conversely, it is extremely important to keep doors and

Preventing basement flooding

If you live on a flood plain, installing a sump pump in your basement in order to drain rising waters in the event of severe flooding will prove a wise investment.

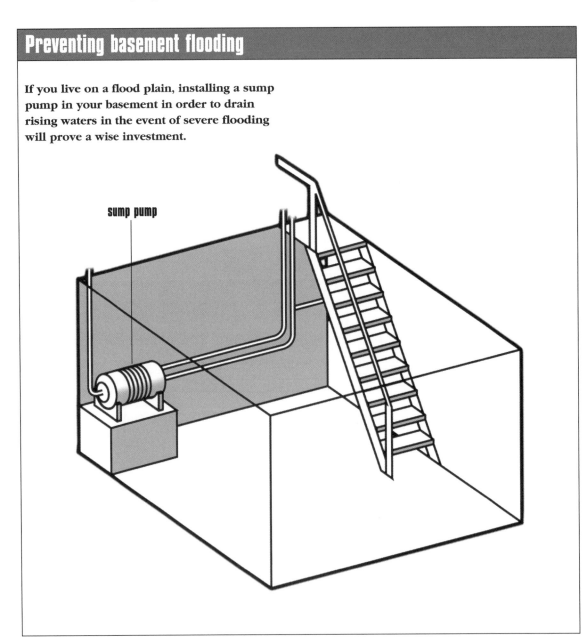

sump pump

windows firmly closed in a storm. Residents of the Gulf of Mexico and Atlantic coasts, where hurricanes and tornadoes are a real threat, should install hurricane shutters on all windows and all doors with glass, and should have all doors fitted with strong locks capable of withstanding force winds.

Many types of manufactured storm shutters are available. Plywood shutters can also be made by measuring each window and each door that has glass and adding 20cm (8in) to both the height and width to provide a 10cm (4in) overlap on each side of the window or door.

For windows 1m (3ft) by 1.2m (4ft) or smaller installed on a wood frame house, it is recommended that you use deep penetrating 6mm ($1/_4$in) lag bolts and plastic-coated permanent anchors. For windows 1m (3ft) by 1.2m (4ft) or smaller installed on a masonry house, 6cm ($1/_4$in) expansion bolts and galvanized permanent expansion anchors are recommended. Larger windows require 1.0cm ($3/_8$in) expansion bolts that penetrate the wall at least 3.8cm ($11/_4$in).

Garage doors

Double-wide garage doors can sometimes be pulled right out of their tracks or collapse in high winds. Extra horizontal bracing can help to reinforce them, in addition to heavier hinges, stronger centre supports, and supplementary bolts.

Making living areas safer

More general precautions around the home are based largely on common sense. Hang heavy pictures and mirrors away from beds, dining tables, or anywhere that people might be sitting or sleeping. You should be able to identify the safest places in your house during a storm or hurricane – such as inner structural walls – and the worst places – in front of windows, or near fireplaces and chimneys. Every family should know and rehearse an emergency plan, including

Hazardous materials

Never store acid and chlorine products side by side. In a major disaster such as an earthquake or tornado, their containers could rupture and mix into a deadly gas.

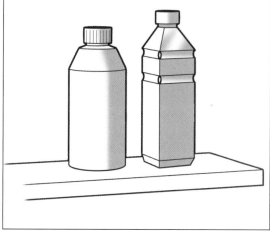

escape routes and meeting places. You should also be able to identify who in your neighbourhood has medical training, and have a plan for reuniting your family should they become separated during a disaster.

COPING WITH HEAVY SNOWFALL

Blizzards are heavy snowstorms with winds in excess of 56km/h (35mph) and temperatures below –6°C (20°F). Winds can reach speeds of more than 72km/h (45mph) and temperatures less than –12°C (10°F). Blizzards often combine high winds with several feet of snow and extreme cold. Other hazards include low visibility, immobilization, and a high potential for hypothermia and frostbite, as well as traffic accidents and the risk of being stranded on the highways.

Blizzards are frequently classified as national emergencies: lake effect blizzards can be especially sudden. By listening to weather forecasts regularly during the

Stormproofing the home

- Brace gabled roofs and install hurricane straps.
- Secure all heavy appliances – water heater, air conditioning unit, and so on.
- Install flexible gas and water connections on all gas appliances.
- Brace chimney and check for loose bricks or fire risk.
- Install and maintain a sump pump system if you have below-grade floors.

- Keep a flashlight and the appropriate tool handy for switching off all utilities – and know how to do so.

- Install latches on all kitchen drawers and cabinets to prevent them flying open in the event of an earthquake.

- Install smoke detectors on every level of your home and near sleeping areas.
- Avoid hanging heavy or glass objects over sleeping or dining areas.

wintertime, you can maintain your own domestic alert status and prepare yourself and your family accordingly.

Remain indoors and conserve energy

During a blizzard, you should stay indoors and out of the cold as much as possible. Avoid excessive heavy physical exertion such as shovelling snow, pushing vehicles, or trying to walk long distances in snowdrifts. Heavy perspiration during extreme cold can lead to chill and hypothermia, and sudden exertion can trigger heart attacks in older or susceptible people. Try to eat high-energy foods such as oatmeal, dried fruit, bread, and peanut butter, and make sure that you drink plenty of hot drinks to maintain your body temperature and fluid intake.

Keeping warm in a power cut

In the event of a power cut, your guiding principle should be extreme caution when attempting to provide alternative heat. Asphyxiation can occur if you use a heating device without the proper ventilation, and thousands of people die needlessly every year as a result of carbon monoxide poisoning. The best way of staying warm safely is to close off unused rooms, stuff towels or rags in the cracks under the doors, and use scrunched-up newspaper for additional insulation. Covering the windows at night in blankets or towels will also help to preserve heat.

You should wear layers of loose-fitting, lightweight warm clothing, as the trapped air between each layer provides added body heat insulation. Wearing a warm hat will help to retain much of the heat lost through your head. At night, you should also wear a hat and sleep under several thinner blankets, rather than one heavy blanket. You should avoid overheating because this could lead to a chill. Eating regularly will also help your body to maintain a steady temperature.

If you must go outside, wear several thin layers for extra insulation, waterproof outer garments, and a hat. Cover your mouth with a scarf to protect your lungs from extreme cold, and wear gloves and watertight boots with textured soles for grip. Watch for fallen power lines or anything sticking out of the snow, and walk cautiously, taking care not to slip and fall.

Preparing for a snowstorm

- Have a snow shovel, flashlights and a battery-operated radio ready.
- Shut off outside water faucets/taps to avoid pipe ruptures and flooding.
- Refuel your car in case you need to drive to a warmer location, and double-check your car's antifreeze.
- Put a shovel, first-aid kit, snowsuit or extra coat, hat, gloves, flashlight, blanket, water, and a safety reflector in your car.
- Make sure that you have all special medications and infant care items on hand in the house.
- Stock up on emergency supplies of water and non-perishable food.
- Purchase a kerosene lantern and camp stove that are safe to use indoors.
- Charge up a cell phone in case phone lines are cut.
- Stock up on salt, extra cat litter, and sand to help keep entranceways passable.

Snowbound in a vehicle

If you find yourself trapped in your car during a snowstorm, remain inside the vehicle. Running the motor for about 10 minutes each hour will provide sufficient heat without running down the car battery, but you must open the window slightly in order to avoid carbon monoxide poisoning. Never attempt to burn anything as a heat source inside the vehicle. Ensure that you are visible to rescuers by turning your lights on intermittently and sounding the horn. Tie a brightly coloured cloth to the antenna of the

If you lose heat in your home

- Seal off any unused rooms by stuffing towels or rags in the cracks under the door.
- Cover the windows with blankets or towels at night.
- Use only devices that are specifically designed for heating indoors as emergency heat sources.
- Ensure proper ventilation when using an alternative-heating device.
- Wear several thin layers and a hat.

Winter car survival kit

- Blankets/sleeping bags
- High-calorie, non-perishable food
- Flashlight with extra batteries
- First-aid kit
- Knife
- Emergency drinking water in bottles
- Extra clothing to keep dry
- Bag of sand (or cat litter) for traction
- Shovel
- Windshield scraper and brush
- Tool kit
- Towrope
- Booster cables

car as a distress signal. Keep the lights on at night, if possible, so that rescue workers are able to find you.

RECOGNIZING AND TREATING HYPOTHERMIA

Frostbite is caused by extreme cold and can permanently damage extremities of the body, such as fingers, toes, nose, and ear lobes. Symptoms are loss of feeling and a white or pale appearance to the skin. Seek immediate medical attention, or slowly rewarm the affected areas. Hypothermia occurs when the body temperature drops to less than 35°C (95°F). Symptoms include slow or slurred speech, incoherence, memory loss, disorientation, uncontrollable shivering, drowsiness, repeated stumbling, and apparent exhaustion.

If the person's temperature falls below 35°C (95°F), immediately seek medical help. Make sure the sufferer is wearing dry clothing, begin warming them slowly, starting with the trunk of the body, and avoid warming extremities (arms and legs) first because sending cold blood towards the heart can lead to heart failure. Cover the head and neck with a warm blanket. Never give alcohol, drugs, or any hot drink or food.

FLOOD RESPONSE

Flooding is caused either by prolonged periods of heavy rainfall or by a sudden heavy storm in areas that lack sufficient

drainage. Urban areas are particularly prone to flooding because land that is covered in roads and parking lots naturally loses its capacity to absorb rainfall. Streets quickly turn into rivers, flood waters rise and enter houses, turning basements and ground floors into death traps. Power lines fall and the city's utilities are usually rapidly affected by flooding and wind damage. Chaos can ensue when drivers are trapped on flooded highways and rescue operations are stalled. The clean-up after a flood is also dangerous, with a high risk of electrocution from damaged utility lines, backed-up sewage, and the risk of infection through polluted flood waters.

Flash flood hazard

One of the more dangerous types of flood is a flash flood, which can occur very suddenly. Nearly half of all flash flood fatalities are vehicle-related because drivers have little time to react. Most flash floods are the result of thunderstorms repeatedly moving over the same area or heavy rains from hurricanes and tropical storms. Flash floods also occur when a dam or a levee bursts or fails, or when an ice jam suddenly releases its water, sometimes resulting in the swift collapse of hillsides, trees, buildings, and bridges.

Most floods are caused by heavy rain from decaying hurricanes or tropical systems, and by rain coupled with melting snows. Coastal floods are caused when tropical storms and hurricanes drive ocean water inland. Coastal flooding is also sometimes caused by sea waves called tsunamis, produced by earthquakes or volcanic activity. Flooding can occur almost anywhere in the world; if it has been raining hard for several hours, or steadily raining for several

Understanding flood alerts

- Flash flooding occurs within six hours of the rain event.
- Flooding is a longer term event and may last a week or more.
- A flood WATCH means a flood is possible in your area: move your furniture and valuables to higher floors of your home. Fill your car's gas tank, in case an evacuation notice is issued.

- A flood WARNING means that flooding is already occurring or will occur soon in your area.
- Listen to local radio and TV stations for information and advice. If told to evacuate, do so as soon as possible.
- A flash flood WATCH means flash flooding is possible in your area: be alert for signs of flash flooding, and be ready to evacuate on a

moment's notice. Avoid driving, particularly in hilly areas with steep inclines or under bridges.
- A flash flood WARNING means that a flash flood is occurring or will occur very soon.
- Evacuate immediately if you are in a high-risk area. Move to higher ground away from rivers, streams, creeks, and low ground.

days, you should tune into your local radio or television stations for weather updates and emergency information.

Caught in a flood

The first rule of thumb during a flood is to go to higher ground and to avoid contact with flood waters. Flood water, even only 15cm (6in) deep, is extremely fast moving and can easily knock you off your feet. As little as 60cm (2ft) of water will float your car, putting your life at risk.

If you are caught in a flood in your car in rapidly rising waters, get out and abandon your car, making your way to higher ground. Never attempt to drive through flooded roadways. If you drive into a flooded area by accident, climb onto the roof of your car and call for help. If you see someone fall into the water, do not attempt to go in after them. Instead, throw the victim a flotation device such as a car seat or plastic bucket, or anything large that will float.

If your house is flooded and you cannot escape from the house to higher unflooded ground without crossing flood waters, make your way to the top of the house to avoid the rising waters. Do not use electricity or gas. If

In a flood warning

- Assemble first-aid kit and essential medications.
- Store drinking water in clean bathtubs and containers; water service may be interrupted.
- Stock up on non-perishable foods.

- Assemble protective clothing – rubber boots, gloves, rainwear.
- Make ready bedding supplies or sleeping bags in case you need to evacuate.
- Ensure you a have battery-powered radio, flashlight,

and extra batteries.
- Keep materials such as sand-bags, plywood, lumber, and garbage bags around in case you need to soak up flood water or build barricades.
- Stay tuned to weather reports.

you are forced to evacuate to your rooftop, be extremely cautious, dress warmly in waterproofs, avoid contact with power lines, and remain visible to air rescue by waving bright articles of clothing.

Precautions in a flooded home

When re-entering a flooded home, be particularly mindful of the potential for electric shock. Contamination is another major threat. Sewage or water that contains particles of decaying animal matter may have washed into houses during a flood. Standing water and wet materials are a breeding ground for microorganisms, such as viruses, bacteria, and mould that cause disease, trigger allergic reactions, and continue to damage materials long after the flood.

You should also be aware of potential chemical hazards such as washed-up propane tanks or spilled acid from car batteries. Ensure that no cuts or wounds are exposed to the air, and wear rubber boots in case of electric shock. A tetanus booster is recommended if

After the flood

- Check and dry out all electrical equipment before it is returned to service.
- When inspecting the flooded home, use flashlights only and never strike a match, in case of a gas leak.
- Throw out all food that has been in contact with flood waters or contaminated air.
- Boil all drinking water before using immediately after the flood, and call your local public health authority to make sure that water is safe to drink.
- Disinfect the house thoroughly, including air conditioning and heating ducts and filters.
- Report damaged utility lines to the appropriate authorities.

Seek higher ground

The rule of all floods is to seek higher ground. In rare cases, this may prove to be the roof of your house. Dress warmly, attract attention with a piece of clothing used as a flag, and avoid power lines.

Response to tornado/hurricane watch

- Prepare by filling your car's tank, and stock up on non-perishable food, water, and batteries.
- Heed the advice of county and state officials regarding evacuations and shelter locations. If you live on the immediate coast, move inland because a tidal wave or potentially fatal flooding could occur.
- Obtain a copy of the evacuation plan advice from a local disaster aid or Red Cross centre.

Disinfect when cleaning

Standing water also poses structural risks to the home, causing floors and ceilings to collapse. Standing water should be removed as quickly as possible. After the water has been removed, the home must be dried out to prevent microorganisms breeding in the damp conditions. When cleaning up, disinfect walls, floors, closets, shelves, and contents of the house using a bleach solution. If heating or air conditioning ducts have been flooded, they must also be disinfected.

Flood waters may wash animals such as snakes into your home or garden. If a snake

it has been more than five years since your last shot. You should not reactivate utilities until you have checked with local utility companies. You may need to have them inspected by a professional first.

In the event of a tornado/hurricane warning

- If you live in a mobile home, evacuate it immediately.
- Close all doors and storm shutters around the house.
- Tie down garden furniture, and put away anything in the vicinity of the house that could become a missile; for example, garden tools.
- Secure sliding doors with wedges in the door track to help prevent the door lifting off in the storm.
- Reinforce garage doors so that they do not fly off and crash into the house.
- Lock and brace trap doors leading to attics to prevent strong winds from swirling through your rafters.
- Take shelter in a 'safe room' or interior room protected by inner walls.
- Remain tuned to the radio for emergency advice and information, and ensure that you have a portable radio in case of a power cut.

Prevent missile damage

Trim back weaker branches from trees to
prevent them being torn off in high winds
and hurled through windows.

Large objects

Move large objects away from doorways where
they could fall and block exits, impeding any
escape or rescue attempts.

bites you, seek immediate medical attention. Do not cut the wound or attempt to suck out the venom.

SURVIVING TORNADOES, HURRICANES, OR SEVERE STORMS

A tornado is a violently rotating column of air extending from a thunderstorm to the ground and reaching wind speeds of 400km/h (250mph) or more, causing damage in excess of 1.6km (1 mile) wide and 80km (50 miles) long. Tornadoes are most common during the spring and summer months. In the United States, an average of 800 tornadoes are reported nationwide each year, killing about 80 people annually. Most people are killed in their cars.

Tornado warning

Signs of a tornado include a build-up of large dark clouds, particularly if greenish-tinted, greenish-tinted skies, large hailstones, heavy rain, strong winds, frequent intense lightning, and – if the tornado is close – a loud roar like the sound of a jet or train. Before a tornado hits, the wind may die down and the air may become very still. Sunlit skies before a tornado are not uncommon. If you notice any such weather signs, stay tuned to weather reports.

Hurricane alert

It is estimated that approximately 75 million people in the United States live within 80km (50 miles) of a potential hurricane zone. Land-falling hurricanes can easily destroy poorly constructed buildings and mobile homes. Most injuries caused during a hurricane are cuts from flying glass or other debris, puncture wounds resulting from exposed nails, metal, or glass, and bone fractures. Hurricanes coming in from the sea usually cause a huge storm surge, or tidal wave, in coastal areas. In the past 30 years, inland flooding has been responsible for more than half the deaths in the United States associated with hurricanes.

When a strike is imminent

If you feel your hair stand on end in the presence of lightning, you are about to be struck and must act immediately. If you cannot jump into a shelter, drop to a crouching position, keeping as low to the ground as possible, yet with as little of your body surface as possible touching the ground.

Find a safe spot

Hurricanes and severe storms bring about a sudden drop in atmospheric pressure, causing buildings to appear to have exploded. Preventing force winds from entering the house is the highest priority when a tornado or hurricane is about to strike. If a tornado or hurricane is imminent, you are safest in your basement or a ground-floor central room surrounded by other rooms protected by innermost walls. Small rooms are sturdier and less likely to collapse, but beware of taking shelter in a room where there is a lot of breakable glass, such as a bathroom. Never take shelter upstairs because wind speeds increase with height above the ground.

If you can take a portable television/radio and flashlight into your shelter space, do so

First aid for lightning casualties

- Check breathing and begin mouth-to-mouth resuscitation if necessary – one breath every 5 seconds for adults and every 3 seconds for small children.
- If the victim is not breathing and has no pulse, cardiopulmonary resuscitation by a trained health professional is necessary.
- Lightning can cause temporary paralysis. Give first aid for shock, and stay with the victim until help arrives.

in order to track the weather updates and evacuation advice. Wear sturdy shoes and extra clothing to protect yourself from broken glass and plaster. To guard against flying shards of glass and metal, wear a hat and cover yourself with blankets, pillows, or coats.

AT RISK FROM LIGHTNING

All major storms produce lightning, and, if you can hear thunder, you are probably close enough to the storm to be struck. Lightning usually strikes the highest object on its way from the sky to the ground, so you should avoid making yourself the tallest object or standing near the tallest object in your immediate area. You should also avoid potential conductors such as wire, metal, and water.

If you are outside, move into a building as fast as possible or into a car with the windows closed. Never stand underneath a tall, isolated tree, and never remain on a motorcycle or bicycle. If you take shelter with other people, make sure that you all stand apart from one another in order to avoid conduction if anyone is struck. If you are inside, you should avoid using the telephone, except for emergencies, and keep away from other electrical appliances such as the television or a radio that could produce a shock.

DANGER FROM FALLEN POWER LINES

After a hurricane or tornado, you should be mindful of fallen power lines in your area. If a power line falls across your car while you are driving, continue to drive away from the line. If the engine stalls, do not turn off the ignition because this could result in a massive electric shock. Stay in your car and wait for emergency personnel. Do not allow anyone other than trained emergency personnel to approach your vehicle because they could be electrocuted while attempting to rescue you.

Check that water is safe

Flooding often occurs with tornadoes and hurricanes, particularly when accompanied by a tidal surge or flooding, and can contaminate the public water supply. After a storm, never assume that the water in your area is safe to drink. Contact the municipal water supplier to check before you wash dishes, brush your teeth, or wash and prepare food. If possible, you should also find out if sewage lines are intact before turning on the water or using the toilet.

If there is flooding in your home, avoid wading in water where broken glass, metal fragments, and other debris may be present. It might also be contaminated. As with any flood clean-up, you will need to dry and disinfect all materials inside the house to prevent the growth of disease-causing moulds.

Check for damage to utilities

You should also be wary of possible structural, electrical, or gas-leak hazards in your home caused by the ravaging effects of a hurricane, tornado or large storm. If you suspect storm damage, do not turn on utilities until a

After a hurricane, tornado or storm

- Do not attempt to move the seriously injured unless they are in immediate danger of further injury.
- Do not turn utilities back on without consulting utility companies and emergency services.
- Avoid any contact with flood water.
- Stay tuned to a portable radio for emergency information and advice.
- Stay out of damaged buildings and beware of buildings collapsing.
- Clean up spilled medicines, bleaches, or gasoline and other flammable liquids immediately.
- Leave the building if you smell gas or chemical fumes.

Building collapse

After an earthquake, be aware of the signs of imminent collapse in a building.

A. Damaged external structures
B. Broken timbers
C and D. Long, deep cracks in the wall
E. Falling plaster

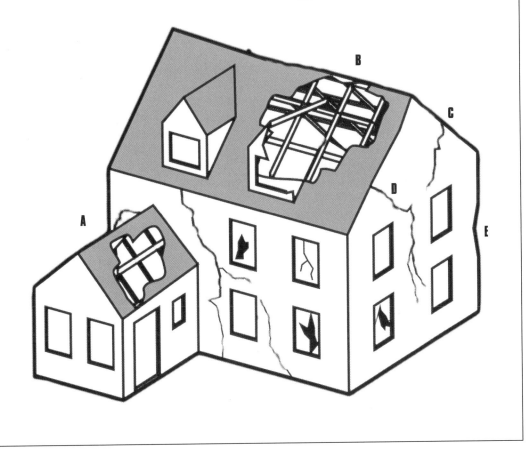

professional service operative from the utility company has inspected your home. Because of the risk of explosion, you should never use candles, gas lanterns, or torches when re-entering a damaged home. If you smell gas or suspect a leak, ensure that the main gas valve is turned off, open all windows to avoid an explosive build-up, and leave the house immediately. Notify the gas company, the police, and fire departments immediately, and do not return to the house until you are told it is safe to do so.

Beware of electrical hazards
Similarly, be mindful about hazardous electrical damage. If you see frayed wiring or sparks when you switch the electricity on, or if you smell burning, immediately shut off the electrical system at the main circuit breaker and consult a certified electrician.

Duck, cover, and hold

In the event of an earthquake, duck down underneath the nearest table, cover your head, and hold on to one of the table legs.

You should prepare to move with the table, keeping its surface above you as cover throughout the quake.

Earthquake drill

- Practise duck, cover, and hold.
- Identify safe areas in every room – sturdy desks and tables, and interior walls.
- Know how to turn off the gas if you can hear or smell a leak.
- Establish an out-of-area contact person who can be called.
- Practise the drill regularly so that habit overcomes fear.
- Plan what you would do if caught in an earthquake when driving.

One of the main reasons for accidental death after a hurricane is fire caused by the careless use of candles in homes without electrical power.

WHEN FOREST FIRES AFFECT URBAN AREAS

Although largely a hazard of southwestern US small towns and outlying suburbs, forest fires have been known to sweep into residential urban areas.

Forest fire urban survival tips
- Avoid wearing synthetic materials, particularly on the feet.

- Soak a large cotton bandanna in water, and tie it around your nose and mouth to filter smoke (do not use synthetic material that could melt).
- Wear a cycling helmet or construction hard hat to protect your hair from the hot embers that fill the skies in all wildfires and from falling debris and branches.
- In a fire, utility lines and telephone poles are often burned. Equip your house with additional supplies of emergency water and non-perishable foods.
- Check that you have a good first-aid kit to hand, containing in particular burns treatment salves.
- Make sure you have a portable radio, flashlight, extra batteries, emergency cooking equipment, fuel, and portable lanterns.

EARTHQUAKE DRILLS AND RESCUE TECHNIQUES

As earthquakes usually occur suddenly without prior warning, drills should be performed regularly in areas affected by quakes. Most public institutions and many employers in earthquake-prone areas have regular earthquake drills. If you do not drill regularly with an organization and you live in an earthquake-prone area, you must ensure your own familiarity with drill basics.

Duck, cover, and hold

The most important safety move during an earthquake is to duck or drop to the floor, take cover under a sturdy desk or table, and hold on to it so that it does not move away from you. You should wait in this position until the shaking stops. This is the famous duck, cover, hold drill, and it is the most important principle of earthquake survival strategy, as you are unlikely to have time for any more elaborate protection. It is important to practise this and to have in mind items of furniture under which you might hide in the event of an earthquake, for example, in your home, your dining room table.

Switch off all heat sources

Other safety tips are worth bearing in mind. As with any major disaster, the risk of fire and flood is high, and you will need to be aware of what to do in such events. An earthquake may interrupt your cooking or other preparations using a heat source, so, if you have a moment to turn off the stove or appliance you are using, doing so could prevent a fire.

Keep away from glass

If an earthquake strikes and you are close to a window, get away from it as soon as possible before ducking and covering. Similarly, stay away from exterior walls, doorways, and lintels, as they are most likely to collapse. Never try to escape by an elevator, and do not panic if fire alarms are activated in the quake. If you are caught in a quake in a public place such as a mall, try to get away from windows, breaking glass, and falling display shelves.

Caught outdoors

If you are caught in a quake outdoors, be careful to avoid power lines, trees, signs, buildings, and other vehicles. If you are driving, try to pull over to the side of the road. Remain inside the vehicle until the quake ends. You will be safest inside your car during a quake: although a car may move around violently during a quake, it nevertheless will afford some additional protection and is a good place to stay until the shaking stops.

If a power line falls on the car, stay inside it and wait for help. After the quake, watch carefully for broken road surface, downed utility poles and wires, and any fallen overpasses and bridges. Remember that you will be in shock, and be prepared to respond to other people's shock symptoms and injuries.

Signs of imminent building collapse

There are several possible causes for a building collapse. Heavy snow can lead to large, older buildings with large, flat expanses of roof

Keeping warm

In the event of losing heat in a severe blizzard, stay in one room, huddle close together, and use all available materials in the house in layers to build up warmth – blankets, curtains, towels, and newspapers. Be sure to stop draughts from entering beneath the door. Make sure that children and the elderly are well covered as they are the most vulnerable.

surface collapsing. A building that has been structurally damaged by a tornado, hurricane, or earthquake is weakened and prone to collapse. Buildings ravaged by fire are extremely susceptible to collapse because their structural integrity is almost always affected.

The most obvious warning of a building about to collapse is the sound of falling plaster or timbers. Any sounds of creaking are also suspect. Dropping ceiling tiles and the sudden appearance of cracks in walls or ceilings are sure signs of structural weakness and should be reported to the building management or local fire department immediately.

If you smell gas, you should get far away from the building. If you are inside the building and suspect collapse, do not use elevators and be particularly wary if you must use staircases in your escape. Never use candles, matches, or lighters after any disaster in case of trapped gas and explosion.

Implosion and explosion
When a building collapses, it will either 'implode' or 'explode'. Implosion, when the building collapses into itself, is likely to be caused when interior weight-bearing structures collapse, pulling exterior walls inwards. Implosion results in extreme depth and density of interior debris and will almost certainly kill, injure, or trap anyone who is inside the building.

Explosion is caused when forces trapped inside rush outwards and, as a result, the surrounding area is covered in debris from the building. Victims are as likely to be buried nearby the building as within it. Immediately after any building collapse, the debris of the building is very unstable and can shift dramatically. Only trained rescue personnel should enter a collapsed building. If you witness a building collapse, you should concentrate on where you last saw people in the building and on informing rescue personnel accurately. Do not attempt to enter a building on the brink of collapse.

Standard kerosene lamp

Kerosene lamps are widely available and can be used indoors in an emergency as a safe alternative lighting source.

RIOTS AND CIVIL UNREST

Cities are prone to periods of civil unrest, particularly when larger populations clash, or when tensions between civil populations and law enforcement officers erupt. When riots flare, they can cause shocking levels of destruction and attract opportunists and looters intent on personal gain. Riots usually reflect years of hostility, and particular ethnic groups may be targeted. Riots can cause demonstrators to behave like urban guerillas – throwing Molotov cocktail bombs, setting cars on fire, looting, and carrying out random beatings.

During the LA riots in 1992, people in the streets were seen throwing rocks, shooting guns, and pulling people from vehicles and beating them. By the time the National Guard was able to subdue the situation, some 54 people had died, 500 fires had been set, and 4500 stores had been destroyed.

Keeping safe

In a riot or period of civil unrest, the streets become a place of almost inevitable danger. Even if you do not believe yourself to be of an ethnicity or type under attack, you may nevertheless find yourself becoming a victim of a robbery or a beating, and police may even attack you. Although you may be curious to witness a news-making event firsthand, going out on the street is extremely foolhardy. You should remain home, and stay away from windows. Do not leave the house for food or water until the period of unrest is under control. Do not try to rescue your car from looters. Stay tuned to the news, and remain equally attuned to events on the street. Be on the alert for fire and flying debris.

After a period of civil unrest or a riot, you should be extremely wary. Avoid areas of broken glass and looted shops, and remain tuned to news information until the situation is completely calmed and under control.

HANDLING FOOD AND FUEL SHORTAGES

If you have prior warning of an impending natural or social disaster, it is wise to stock up on non-perishable food items. If power is out, you will no longer be able to rely on a refrigerator. You can eat the contents of the refrigerator on the day power goes out, but avoid eating non-refrigerated meat or dairy

Emergency kit

Keep these items in an easy-to-reach place in your home, ready for an emergency situation. Ensure that batteries are fresh and that they fit your radio and flashlight.

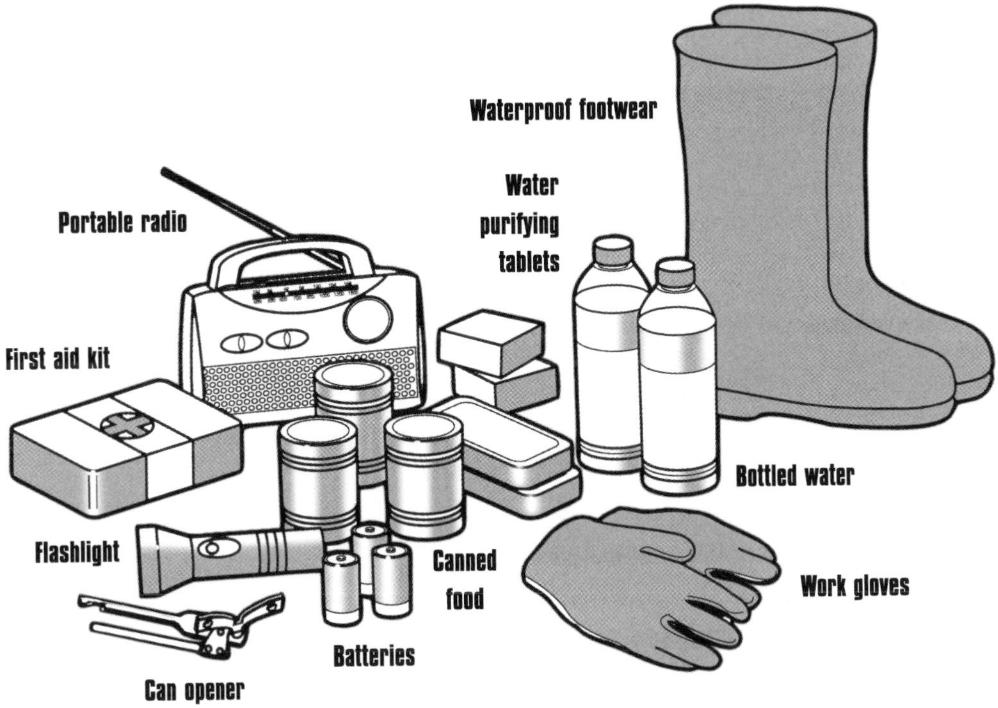

Waterproof footwear

Water purifying tablets

Portable radio

First aid kit

Bottled water

Flashlight

Canned food

Work gloves

Batteries

Can opener

products thereafter. Clearly the kinds of food to stock up on are those that do not require heating or the addition of water. For this reason, canned foods are usually the most convenient, especially protein-rich foods such as beans, fish, and meat. Many canned foods are high in salt, however, and should not be eaten for long periods of time. Dried oatmeal, dried fruit, and unsalted nuts are a good alternative. Canned milk, UHT milk, and evaporated milk can be used in place of fresh milk and can be stockpiled for many

months. Canned fruits such as grapefruit or other citrus fruits will provide vitamin C. Peanut butter is a good source of protein and energy yielding fats.

In a fuel shortage, you may be forced to rely on a portable stove. The best choice is a kerosene or propane stove designed for safe use indoors. Read the manufacturer's instructions carefully, and ensure adequate ventilation. Never bring an outdoor grill indoors or use any other appliance where there is a risk of fire or carbon monoxide poisoning. Only use a wood-burning stove or fireplace if you are sure that it is clean and in working order.

Emergency electricity, light, heat and water

It is common for utility supply to be cut during a major natural or social disaster. If you are no longer able to use electricity, gas, or water, your main concerns will quickly be staying warm and avoiding dehydration.

Generating electricity is not usually an option. Home generators are not always particularly efficient, are expensive to obtain and run, and can give off dangerous fumes. In a true emergency, you may consider using your car battery's reserve capacity. This will supply about 10 amps for 3 hours or so, and at least allow you to remain tuned to a radio.

Follow safety instructions

If you plan to use a wood stove, fireplace, or space heater for heat, be careful to avoid fire hazards and to ensure adequate ventilation,

Three ways to purify water

- **BOILING**
  The safest method. Boil for 3–5 minutes.
- **DISINFECTION**
  Use 16 drops of unscented household liquid bleach per 4.5 litres (1 gallon) of water, stir, and let stand for 30 minutes. Use only liquid bleach containing 5.25 per cent sodium hypochlorite. Never use colour-safe or scented bleaches, or bleaches with added cleaners.
- **DISTILLATION**
  Half-fill a saucepan with water. Tie a cup to the saucepan's lid on the inside so that the cup dangles inside the saucepan with the lid covered, just above the water but not touching it. Let the water boil for 20 minutes – the cup will fill with the water that drips from the inside of the lid.

especially when using a kerosene heater. Never attempt to use a substitute fuel for your portable heater, only the type recommended by the manufacturer, and follow all safety instructions carefully. Do not use the heater if it has a damaged electrical cord or produces sparks. Only use fireplaces or wood stoves if they are properly maintained, vented to the outside, and do not leak flue gas into the indoor air space. Chimney fires are another major cause of house fires. Be sure to clear the hearth of combustible material, and avoid using green or damp wood, which will result in polluting and potentially dangerous levels of smoke.

Live in one room

Although you may need to provide a heating unit with ventilation, the best way of keeping warm in a house without central heating is to close off a room and have all occupants in the house use only this room. Stuff towels or newspaper in cracks under doors, and hang blankets over the windows in addition to the curtains or drapes. Dress warmly in several layers. Eating regular meals will help you to stay warmer, and drinking regularly is almost equally important. However, avoid alcohol because, although it may make you feel warm initially, it will cause your body to lose heat rapidly afterwards and can lead to chills.

Opt for kerosene or paraffin lighting

Rely on daylight, then use battery-powered flashlights rather than candles if possible, to reduce the risk of fires. Never leave lit candles unattended. Kerosene lanterns or lamps that run on paraffin oil will run for long periods of time – as much as 45 hours on one filling. Make sure that you have a fire extinguisher handy and that battery-operated smoke alarms are installed.

When water is in short supply

Dehydration, caused by lack of adequate water supply, can quickly lead to serious illness,

Emergency water supply

Ensuring that you have an adequate supply of drinking water during a natural or social disaster is vital. Prepare by filling baths, hand basins, sinks, and every available bottle and bowl with water. Water in the hot water tank and toilet tank (though not in the toilet bowl) may be purified as drinking water and ice in the freezer can also be used as a water source.

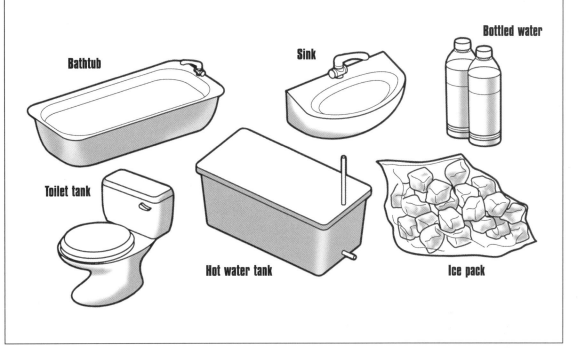

Bathtub

Sink

Bottled water

Toilet tank

Hot water tank

Ice pack

particularly in the case of the very young, elderly, or infirm. A normally active person needs to drink at least 285ml (10 fl oz) of water each day, and children, nursing mothers, and those who are sick need even more.

Store a total of at least 4.5 litres (8 pints) per person, per day. If disaster strikes suddenly, you may be forced to use emergency water supplies around the house, such as the water in your hot-water tank, pipes, and ice cubes. As a last resort, you can use water in the reservoir tank – not the bowl – of your toilet. To use the water in your pipes, let air into the plumbing by turning on the faucet/tap in your home at the highest level, allowing a small amount of water to trickle out and drain from the lowest faucet in the house. To use the water in your hot-water tank, turn off the water intake valve to start water flowing, and turn on a hot-water faucet.

To ensure that the microorganisms that cause dysentery, typhoid fever, and hepatitis A do not contaminate these emergency water supplies, you should purify all water before using it to drink.

Emergency outdoor sources of water should be treated with extreme caution and always purified before use. These include rainwater, collected in a clean container, ponds and lakes, and natural springs. Never drink flood water, and avoid all standing water and any water that is dark and strong smelling.

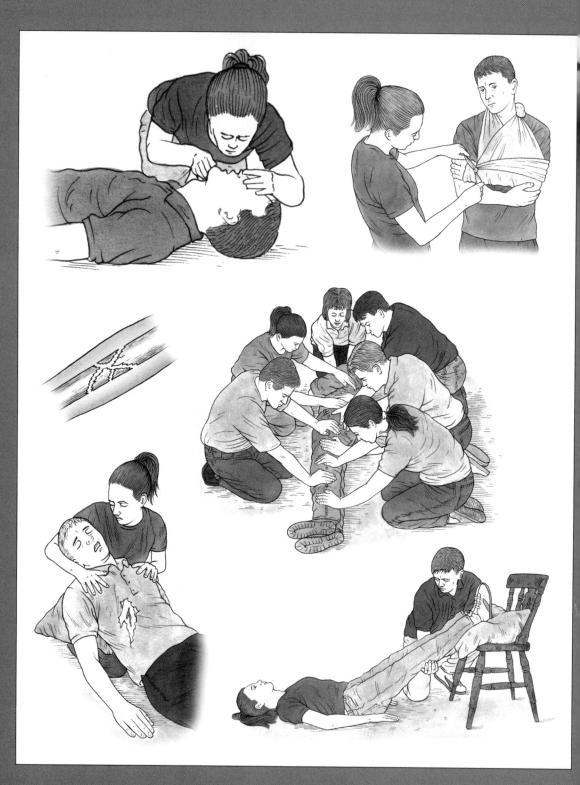

CHAPTER EIGHT

Administering first aid

First aid is the treating of an injured or sick person prior to the arrival of professional medical assistance. Except in cases of minor injuries, urban first aid is never a substitute for treatment by a doctor or paramedic.

However, this may not be the case in an isolated natural setting. Here the first aider may have to sustain treatment over a long period of time until rescue arrives. The only realistic possibility of this occurring in an urban setting is in a major civil emergency when medical services are swamped to the point where rapid-response services collapse.

This chapter describes how to carry out essential first-aid treatments for significant or life-threatening injuries. However, it cannot be emphasized strongly enough that, for a rounded, confident practice of first aid, it is essential to take a good course in the subject. Use only reputable first-aid training agencies belonging to accredited national bodies.

VITAL FUNCTIONS

On encountering an injured or ill person, a first aider has one initial priority above all others – treat any impairment of the victim's vital functions. The human body has three major systems of concern to the first aider: the circulatory system, the respiratory system, and the nervous system.

CIRCULATORY SYSTEM

The circulatory system is responsible for pumping oxygenated blood around the body. It consists of the heart and a network of arteries and veins running from head to toes. The heart is the engine for the whole process of blood circulation. Deoxygenated blood is drawn into the heart, then pumped towards the lungs via the pulmonary artery. The blood is oxygenated from the lungs and returned to the heart. Oxygenated blood is then pumped out around the rest of the body via the arteries. (Arteries are responsible for carrying oxygenated blood away from the heart, while veins carry deoxygenated blood towards the heart.)

Essential blood supply

Human blood has many critical biological functions, but for the first aider the oxygenation of the body is the most important. As blood passes through the circulatory system, it relinquishes its oxygen content into body tissues. Without this oxygen, most body tissues begin to deteriorate and die very quickly. The brain is acutely vulnerable to oxygen deprivation, and, with no blood supply to the brain, a person may well die within two minutes.

The circulatory system can be damaged or impaired in any number of ways. The most common problems are:

- Loss of blood through an injury, possibly resulting in shock (a critical reduction in blood volume leading a lowering of blood pressure and ineffective circulation).
- Inadequate oxygenation (which is known as hypoxia) of the body, usually stemming from problems with the respiratory system.
- Problems with heart function such as a heart attack or thrombosis.

RESPIRATORY SYSTEM

The respiratory system is responsible for drawing in air from the outside world, extracting the oxygen and passing it into the blood, then expelling waste gases. It consists of the mouth, nose, trachea, lungs. and a network of arteries and capillaries used to achieve the blood/oxygen transfer.

Air is drawn into the lungs through the nasal passages and trachea. The trachea subdivides into two tubes as the bronchi, each feeding into a lung sac. Inside the sacs, the bronchi continually subdivide into smaller and smaller air passages, terminating in millions of microscopic air sacs called alveoli. Oxygen passes from the alveoli into the bloodstream through tiny capillaries. Carbon dioxide – the main gas left over after air has been processed – is expelled from the lungs when we breathe out.

Naturally, any respiration problem is serious, as without proper respiration body oxygenation is impaired. First-aid emergencies involving the respiratory system can be wide ranging and include: obstructed airways, injuries to the lungs or chest, allergic reactions affecting breathing, heart attacks (these often result in the cessation of breathing), oxygen deprivation in the environment (such as inhaling smoke), and even head injuries that damage brain areas responsible for breathing.

NERVOUS SYSTEM

The nervous system is effectively the motor of the human body. Its duties are extremely broad, ranging from thought processes and emotional responses through to regulating vital functions such as breathing and heart rate. The brain performs the majority of these duties, but the nervous system also includes the spinal column and a large network of nerves transmitting impulses around the body. The spinal column is particularly crucial. Effectively, it is the main power line for the nervous system. Damage to it through spinal injury can result in anything from paralysis to instant death – hence the acute levels of caution exercised by emergency crews when treating back injuries.

The nervous system is exposed to damage from both external and internal sources. Externally, head injuries or spinal injuries are the main concern. Internally, the brain is susceptible to diseases, such as meningitis, or biological assaults, such as strokes and epilepsy. Imbalances in blood-sugar levels, typically resulting from diabetes, also affect nervous function and consciousness.

MAKING A DIAGNOSIS

Understanding the three vital systems of the human body is invaluable for the initial stage of first-aid treatment: diagnosis. The ABC method of diagnosis, explained below, is the quickest route to ascertaining if any of the vital systems are threatened or injured, and also the most easily remembered at an accident. Knowing what is going on in the body and how the systems are linked can also prepare the first aider for possible complications arising from the original injury.

Checking for breathing and opening the airway

Open the casualty's airway by tilting the head slightly backwards using two fingers under the chin. Check that the airway is not obstructed. Place your cheek by the casualty's open mouth, and look along the chest. If you cannot hear or feel breath, and cannot observe the normal rise and fall of the chest, the casualty may need mouth-to-mouth resuscitation.

There are two main responsibilities in first-aid diagnosis: 1) to gain a basic insight into what is wrong; and 2) to acquire as much information as possible about the illness or injury to assist the emergency services when they arrive. The first part traditionally applies the ABC method. The three letters stand for airway, breathing, and circulation, and explain the order in which the casualty's vital signs should be checked.

- **Airway** – look in the casualty's mouth and remove anything obstructing the windpipe, such as false teeth, vomit, or food. Also pull the tongue forwards. The tongue of an unconscious person can flop to the back of the mouth and block the airway.
- **Breathing** – place your cheek just over the casualty's mouth and nose while looking down the body at the chest and resting your hand on the breastbone. If the respiratory system is functioning normally, you should feel warm breath on your cheek and hear the breathing; you should also see or feel the chest rising and falling. Be cautious that external influences such as high winds, loud noises, and thick clothing do not lead you to make a misdiagnosis.
- **Circulation** – check that the casualty has a pulse. The best place to check for a pulse is along the throat. Run the fingers (but not the thumb) from beneath the ear along the line of the jaw. Continue downwards until the fingers rest in the soft hollows of the throat just beneath the jaw line and either side of the windpipe. You should feel a pulse.

An alternative is the radial pulse in the wrist. This is located on the inner wrist between the thumb-side of the arm and the prominent tendon, which runs down from the hand. Check for the pulse using the fingers, never the thumb. The thumb has its own pulse, which may confuse your diagnosis. Whichever place you source the pulse, if the pulse is weak or absent for more than 10 seconds, the circulatory system is impaired.

Check the whole body

The ABC procedure should lead you to the most serious issues straight away and enable you to make life-saving treatments. Refine your diagnosis further by looking for the cause. Check the body carefully from top to toe. Feel gently for any hidden injuries; look for any obvious points of blood loss; note any heavy swellings or bruisings, particularly to the head, spine, abdomen, or chest. Examine the lips and fingernails – if they are turning blue or are very pale, circulation is poor.

Gather information

Alongside your medical diagnosis, carry out historical and environmental diagnoses. Find out as much as possible about the accident or illness using the casualty, witnesses, or relatives as references. Also try to discover the casualty's name and address. Note the time of an accident. Perform regular ABC checks, and note the time of any changes in the results. Look for clues about an incident in the surrounding world. If poisoning is suspected, for example, try to collect a sample of the poison for the medical crews, if you can do so safely.

Search an unconscious person for any indicators of prior medical conditions. Evidence includes tablets, syringes, a medical bracelet, or medical card. Your aim is to gather as much information as possible. When emergency crews arrive, tell them what you have discovered quickly and without embellishment.

RESUSCITATING A CASUALTY

If the ABC diagnosis reveals that breathing or heartbeat has stopped, then the first aider must attempt to restore or support the basic functions of respiration and circulation. To

Cardiopulmonary resuscitation (CPR)

The object of CPR is to work the casualty's respiration and circulation manually until he either regains these functions himself or the emergency services arrive. Ideally, CPR should be performed by two people working in tandem and frequently swapping roles, as the process is physically exhausting for one person to maintain over any length of time.

(C) Check the casualty's pulse by placing two fingers just beneath the angle of the jawline to the side of the windpipe. If no pulse (hence no heartbeat) is detected, proceed to steps D and E.

(A) Lay the casualty down and check their level of consciousness. If they are conscious and talking, then CPR is not required.

(D) Open the airway, pinch the casualty's nose, seal your mouth around the casualty's, and exhale fully. Your breath should make the casualty's chest rise. Take your mouth away, and allow the chest to fall naturally before repeating the process.

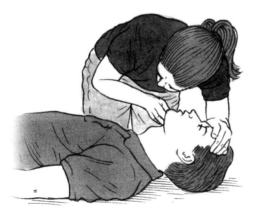

(B) Check if the casualty is breathing. If there is no sign of breathing for 10 seconds, proceed to steps C and D.

(E) After two breaths, switch to chest massage. Make 15 quick compressions of the breast-bone, pushing down to a depth of around 4–5cm (1.5–2in) on an adult. Check the vital signs, and repeat CPR as necessary.

make matters more demanding, if one system stops, the other usually joins it.

Cardiopulmonary resuscitation (CPR) involves the first aider manually breathing for the casualty and applying external pressure to the heart to keep blood moving around the circulatory system. The external heart massage and breathing technique in a mutually supportive role are described below, but they can be used individually if only one system is affected. If no pulse or breathing is detected for at least 10 seconds, first open the casualty's airway. With the casualty on their back, place two fingers just under the point of the chin, and lift the jaw while gently tipping the head backwards. (Note: do not tip the head too far back if there is a possibility that the casualty has a spine or neck injury.) This action lifts the tongue off the back of the throat ready for artificial respiration (AR).

Mouth-to-mouth ventilation

AR involves breathing for the casualty until their respiration is restored or professional medical help arrives. Holding the head in the tilted position, check once again that the airway is clear of obstructions. Next, pinch the casualty's nostrils together, and place your mouth over theirs, making a tight seal with the lips. Blow into the mouth for about 2 seconds, hard enough to make the casualty's chest rise, then remove the lips and let the chest fall back to its natural position. Do this once, and check for a pulse. If the pulse remains absent, proceed to full CPR. If circulation does return, keep repeating mouth-to-mouth ventilation, but check the pulse every 10 breaths. Finally, should breathing return (usually preceded by coughing, swallowing, and so on), place the casualty in the recovery position (see box feature).

CPR alternates chest compressions with mouth-to-mouth ventilation. While ventilation can put oxygen into the lungs, oxygenated blood will not travel around the body unless cardiac massage is used. Chest compressions

work by pushing down on the breastbone, which in turn squeezes the heart against the backbone and forces blood out around the circulatory system. On release, the chest rises and blood is sucked back into the heart ready to be expelled by the next compression.

Chest compressions

This first aider demonstrates the correct position for delivering chest compressions. The fingers are interlocked, meaning that both hands push in the same spot, while the lower hand provides a cushion for the thrust to reduce the risk of breaking ribs. The woman is leaning directly over the casualty with the arms practically straight. This position allows her to use her whole body weight in the compressions against the resistance of the breastbone.

Carrying out CPR

First, kneel at the side of the casualty. Run a finger up one of the lowest ribs until it stops in the centre of the chest. A finger's width above this point is the lower breastbone, the point of the compressions. Mark this place with a finger, then place the heel of the hand here, thumb edge of the heel touching against the finger. Without moving the heel position, take the first hand and place it on top of the other hand, interlocking the fingers. Lean over the casualty with straightened arms. To make a

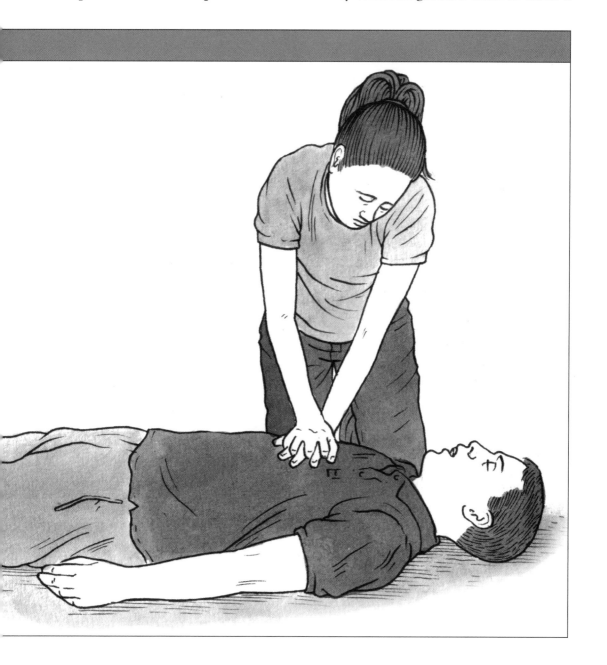

Elevating bleeding limbs

It is important to stem major blood loss as soon as possible. Raising a bleeding limb reduces the blood pressure to that limb and hence reduces the speed of the blood loss. At the same time, apply compression to the wound to encourage clotting. Try to calm the casualty as much as possible – the lower the heart rate, the lesser the bleeding.

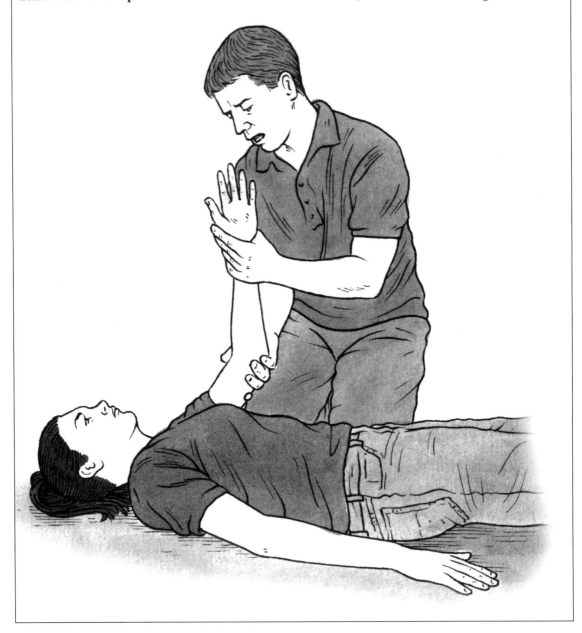

Bandaging around an embedded object

Do not attempt to remove any object that is deeply embedded in flesh – pulling it out can cause serious bleeding and damage tissue. Instead, press either side of the object to control the immediate bleeding before bandaging around the object to prevent further infection and stabilize the object against further movement.

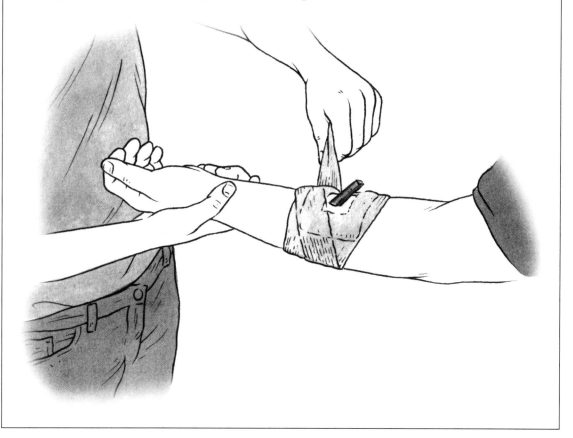

single compression, push down quickly on the breastbone to a depth of around 4–5cm (1.5–2in), then release the pressure. Repeat this action 15 times, alternating with two breaths of artificial ventilation. The whole process is exhausting. If possible get another first aider to perform one of the elements, and switch roles regularly. Otherwise, there is the danger that you might pass out from making the repeated breaths or that your chest compressions will become weak and ineffectual.

Maintaining CPR
The best result of CPR is to restore the casualty's breathing and circulation. Check vital signs regularly (after every one or two CPR cycles). If they return, place the casualty in the recovery position; keep under close observation until help arrives. If not, maintain CPR until help arrives. If help does not arrive within 30 minutes, the possibilities of maintaining CPR are restricted. You will be truly exhausted. In addition, if a person does not

Treating a chest injury

Chest injuries may indicate a punctured lung, particularly if the casualty is in respiratory distress and frothy blood is bubbling out of his mouth. Support the casualty in an upright position, leaning towards the injured side – this helps any internal bleeding drain away from the healthy lung.

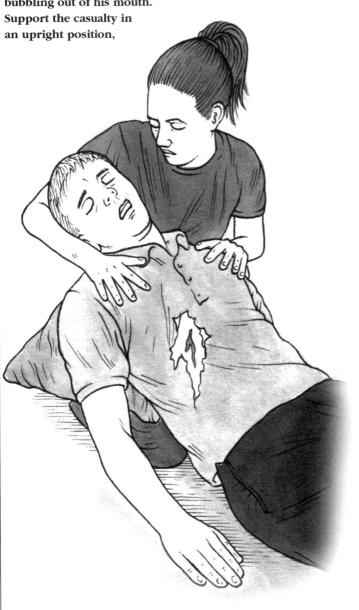

respond to CPR within that time limit, they are unlikely to respond to further treatment. These factors, when combined with other information about injuries, may lead you to stop (such as massive blood loss or severe trauma to the head or chest).

Treating circulatory sh

Circulatory shock is a life-threatening drop in blood pressure caused by loss of body fluids or blood. The main first-aid treatment for shock involves stopping the fluid loss – usually bleeding – and elevating and supporting the casualty's legs. Raising the legs reduces blood flow to these large limbs and concentrates available blood around the vital organs in the torso.

WOUNDS AND BLEEDING

Wounds range from minor and almost painless injuries to major life-threatening trauma. Your priority as a first aider is to prevent major blood loss affecting the circulatory system. If an adult loses more than 1 litre (2 pints) of blood, their blood pressure drops to unsafe levels – a condition known as circulatory shock, or volume shock. Normal blood pressure is required to perform the efficient oxygenation of blood, so the blood loss must be stemmed. After 2 litres (4 pints) of blood loss, the casualty will probably lose consciousness; at 3 litres (6 pints), there is a strong chance of cardiac arrest and death. Signs of circulatory shock include rapid and weak pulse, shallow and fast breathing, a bluing of the skin in the face, and a sweaty complexion.

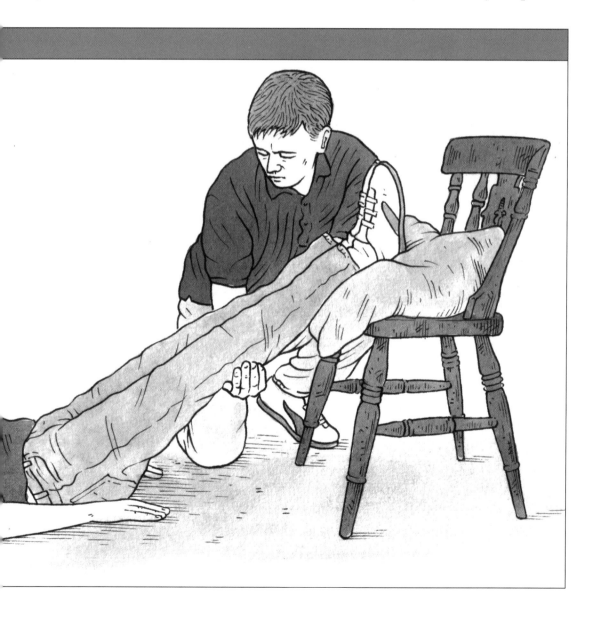

Apply pressure to a wound

Almost all first aid responses for bleeding follow the same simple procedure. Lay the casualty down, and remove any clothing around the wound site, exposing the injury. Apply strong direct pressure to the wound. Ideally, you should use a thick wad of clean material, but if this is not available then even your bare hand will do. If an object is embedded in the wound, place the pressure around the object and not on top. Maintain a firm pressure, placing new pads of material over the first if it becomes soaked with blood.

Applying pressure stems further blood loss by assisting the natural process of blood clotting. In the case of limb injuries, elevate the limb to reduce blood pressure to wound area and make blood loss easier to control. If the bleeding appears to be stopping, bandage the dressing in place over the wound and take the casualty to the emergency services.

More serious wounds

The bleeding from most minor wounds can be controlled fairly successfully through this method. Multiple or major wounds prove more of a problem. In cases of multiple bleeding injuries, you should concentrate on the more serious wounds. The most critical bleeding comes from severed arteries or veins. Arterial bleeding is characterized by bright red, oxygenated blood pumping out of the wound at pressure, even jetting several feet into the air. Venous (from the veins) bleeding is dark red in colour (the blood has given up its oxygen content) and does not have the same pressure, but can still gush from a major wound. Target these types of bleeding for your immediate attention.

Abdominal and chest wounds

These serious wounds also require special consideration. The same pressure-then-bandage procedure is applied, but the positioning of the casualty's legs is important. If the wound runs across the abdomen, raise the knees and support them with something like a rolled-up coat. This takes pressure off the injury site. If, however, the wound runs vertically down the abdomen, keep the legs flat. Should the abdominal contents issue from the wound, hold them in place with a sterile dressing. If the intestines protrude, try to wrap the exposed parts in a clean plastic bag or kitchen film wrap, so that they do not dry out in the atmosphere.

Penetrating chest injuries are particularly serious. Air or blood entering the chest cavity can cause the lungs to collapse, or the lung itself may be punctured. Symptoms of such conditions include circulatory shock, coughing up frothy, red blood, blood bubbling up out of the wound, a crackly sensation in the skin of the chest, and the sound of air being drawn into the wound on inhalation.

How to help prevent infection

The goal of first-aid treatment is to assist respiration and prevent airborne bacteria being drawn into the chest cavity. Stop immediate bleeding through the usual method. When bleeding is under control, place a clean dressing over the wound and surrounding area. Next, cover the pad with an airtight material, such as a plastic bag, kitchen film wrap or kitchen foil. Tape this in place on three sides only. In effect, you have constructed an elementary one-way valve. When the casualty breathes in, the valve closes over the wound to stop the ingress of air. When he breathes out, the open side of the valve allows the air to be released.

As a final measure, lean the casualty towards the injured side of his chest. This allows blood within the chest cavity to drain away from the healthy lung.

Internal bleeding

This category of bleeding is insidious, as it may present no outward signs, but can result in circulatory shock, just like external bleeding. It results from a number of causes. Fractures,

Preventing heat loss

Heat loss presents a significant danger to casualties who are suffering from circulatory shock or severe burns, or who are unavoidably exposed to the elements while waiting for the emergency services. Cover the casualty, and, if possible, place some warm material between them and the ground – more body heat will be lost into the ground than into the air. Also try to make sure that the head, hands, and feet are well insulated.

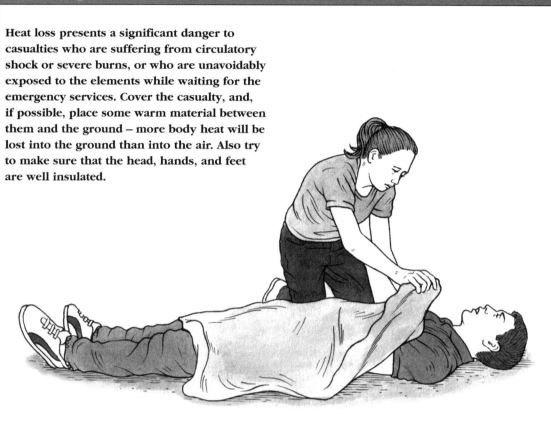

penetrating wounds, or heavy contusions may open up internal wounds, as may medical conditions such as stomach ulcers.

Signs of internal bleeding are usually a deterioration in the casualty's mental condition (such as confusion or disorientation), unconsciousness, internal pains, thirst, and cold and clammy skin with a loss of skin colour. There may also be bleeding from orifices. In general, the treatment for internal bleeding and circulatory shock is the same.

Raise the legs

Lie the casualty down, ideally on a blanket or a piece of material, to protect them from the cold ground. Loosen clothing around the neck, chest, and waist. Elevate the legs as high as possible and support them. By raising the limbs, you are allowing as much blood as possible to remain in the torso, where it can be used by the body's vital organs. Constantly check the casualty's vital signs for any deterioration in condition, and be prepared to deliver CPR if necessary.

BURNS

As well as those from fire, artificial heat sources, and hot water, there are several other forms of burn. Sunburn is one of the most readily experienced and can be serious if allowed to reach critical levels. Chemical burns result from the reaction of the skin with strong acids, alkalis, or industrial chemicals. A powerful electric shock will usually leave a substantial burn at the point of contact. Friction burns are caused by heat build-up generated by movement between the skin and an object, while inhaling abnormally heated air or caustic gases, often in the presence of an actual blaze, causes respiratory burns.

Lastly, even cold can cause burns. Touching a freezing piece of metal, for instance, may result in a nasty localized burn.

Degrees of danger

Burns are graded according to their depth. The depth of a burn is described by the 'degree' system. A first-degree burn does only superficial damage to the surface of the skin, resulting in redness and swelling, but little need for treatment. Second-degree burns have damaged the outer layer of skin known as the epidermis. These burns are painful and usually require first aid or more advanced medical treatment. Signs of damage include pain, swelling, skin flaking, and blistering. While not serious if they cover a limited area, if more than 60 per cent of the body receives second-degree burns, the injury could be fatal.

Third-degree burns are the most dangerous level. The heat of the burn sears down through the epidermis and underlayer of skin, the dermis, which contains nerves, hair follicles, muscles, and sweat glands. Sometimes a third-degree burn can even go through the dermis and reach the layer of fatty tissue beneath. Third-degree burns look as serious as they are. Skin is charred black or grey; bones and muscles may be exposed. Such injuries are life-threatening. In response to burns, the body's blood vessels divert fluid to the burn site. With major burns, the fluid loss can be so extreme that the casualty enters into volume shock.

Treating burns

There is a standard procedure for treating burns to the skin, with variations according to the severity of the burn. First, remove the patient from the heat source. If their clothes

Cooling a burn

Burns should be cooled as soon as possible to alleviate the damage caused by heat transference through the tissue. Ideally, clothing should be removed before pouring copious amounts of cold water over the wound. If the clothing is burnt onto the wound, leave it in place (attempting to remove it will tear the damaged and fragile skin), and pour the water over the clothing instead.

are on fire, smother the flames by wrapping the person in a piece of material or making them roll on the ground. Do not put yourself in danger. Be especially wary of entering burning buildings on a rescue mission. Even if there are no flames in the immediate vicinity, superheated air and poisonous gases can kill with terrifying rapidity. The air temperature alone in a house fire can reach that of a small industrial blast furnace.

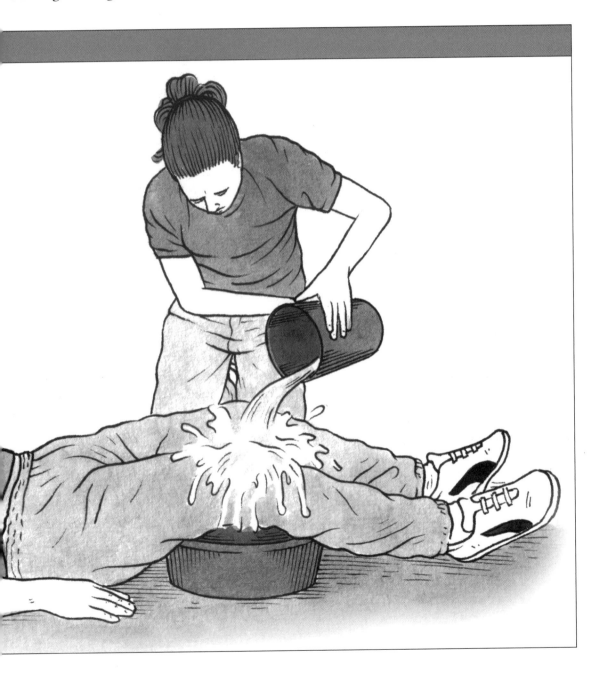

Once in a safe position, begin treatment. Remove restrictive items of jewellery or clothing from around the burn area. Cut away clothing rather than remove it conventionally if the burn is severe. However, if the clothing or anything else is sticking to the flesh, do not remove it. Taking it off will tear the skin even more and expose the casualty to chronic infection.

How to cool the burn

A burn does its work by transferring heat into the skin tissue, and the heat will continue to do damage for some time if it is not counteracted. Do this by pouring cold water over the injury for at least 10 minutes, increasing to 20 minutes in the case of a chemical burn. If you have had to leave the clothing on, keep soaking the material over the burn.

Be careful about the dangers of over-cooling the casualty. If a high percentage of the body is burned, cooling it may lower the casualty's body temperature to the point of inducing hypothermia.

Other cautions include:

- Never burst any blisters present – doing so will expose the casualty to further infection.
- Do not touch the wound more than necessary.
- Do not apply lotions, creams, fats, or other substances to the burn.
- Once the wound is cooled, it then requires dressing (ideally, by now the emergency services will be on their way). For minor burns, cover with a sterile dressing and bandage in place as for any type of wound. If bandages are not available, a plastic bag or kitchen film wrap will provide good temporary protection from airborne bacteria, and can be easier to use on large-scale severe burns.
- Once the wound is dressed, monitor the casualty for signs of shock while waiting

for the emergency services to arrive. Keep a close check on breathing and pulse rate, and note any significant changes.

In two distinct cases, first-aid treatment for burns varies from the above:

- **Chemical burns** – treat as for a normal burn, but protect yourself from contamination with protective clothing (improvised out of plastic bags if necessary) and a face mask. If the chemical is in the victim's eye, irrigate the eye with cold water, but do not let the water flow across the good eye or near the casualty's mouth.
- **Respiratory burns** – as with internal burns, these cannot be treated with irrigation. Signs of respiratory burns include a burnt or sooty face and respiratory difficulty. There is little you can do apart from remove the casualty to a place of fresh air, loosen any tight clothing from around the neck and chest, and monitor breathing in case it becomes life-threatening.

INJURIES TO BONES AND JOINTS

Human bones and joints are impressively durable. Substantial impact, however, can fracture bones or dislocate joints. Apart from injuries to the skull and head, in strict medical terms bone and joint injuries are not too serious. Even the most devastated bone can often be repaired by surgery. What causes problems is often the damage the broken bone does to surrounding tissue and blood vessels, particularly if the bone is in the middle of a major muscle group. A broken thighbone, for example, can severe the femoral artery and lead to massive, possibly fatal, bleeding.

Types of fractures

Broken bones come in several types, but the first aider faces two main categories: open and closed fractures. An open fracture is one in which the sharp end of the broken bone has pierced the skin. Signs of an open fracture are obvious. As well as heavy bruising and swelling, the bone will be visible through the skin, and there may be heavy bleeding. A closed fracture means the break is contained within the skin. Heavy swelling and bruising around the break area and possibly an unusual angle in a limb will indicate the break. The signs of joint dislocation are similar to those of a closed fracture, though located around a joint area.

All fractures and dislocations usually result in chronic pain, severe difficulty with movements, and nausea. Fractures can even result in fatalities if the broken bone severs an artery, resulting in major internal bleeding. Signs of shock may develop, particularly if the fracture is located in the thighbone, pelvis, or ribcage. To ensure you are dealing with fracture or dislocation, try to find out what happened to the cause the injury. If anyone was present at the accident, did the casualty suffer a heavy blow or fall? Was there a snapping sound at point of impact? Which part of their body took the main force of the impact?

Steady, support, immobilize

The basic treatment for fractures and dislocations is summed up by the words 'steady, support, immobilize'.

- **Steady** – make the casualty stay still and lie down if possible. If the fracture is open, treat for bleeding with the method described above. Place pads of material around the exposed bone until you can bandage gently over it.
- **Support** – if you are dealing with a broken or dislocated limb, restrict its movement as much as possible. Movement of broken bones can cause further damage to muscles and blood vessels. First support the limb by holding it steady on the ground or against another stable surface. This procedure in itself may be sufficient until professional help arrives.

Types of fracture

Simple fracture – the bone is broken cleanly, usually caused by a heavy blow to a single, defined point.

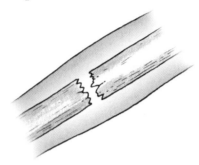

Comminuted fracture – the bone is shattered into multiple fragments, making it difficult to set and repair.

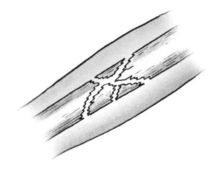

Greenstick fracture – the bone is split partway through its width. This injury tends to occur in children, who have softer and more flexible bones than adults.

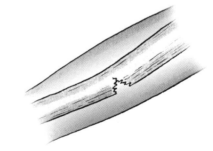

Arm sling

This type of bandage is used to support a fractured arm or elbow. A basic sling is made by looping a broad piece of material under the damaged arm and tying it around the back of the neck. An extra bandage is then taken around the torso and tied just above the supported wrist. This bandage immobilizes the arm against the chest to prevent it swinging while walking.

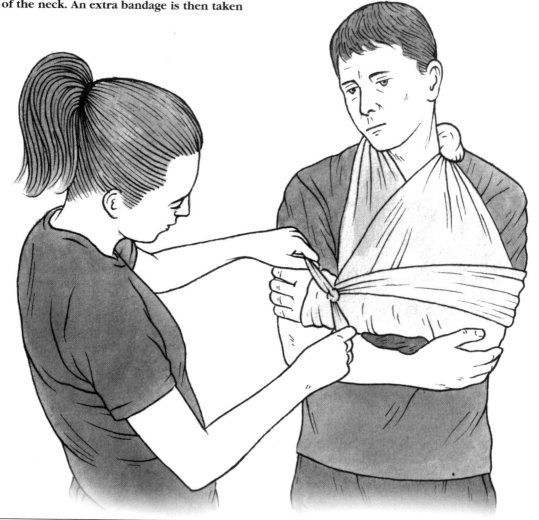

- **Immobilize** – if, however, you need to move the casualty to a treatment area or away from an accident site, you will need to make the immobilization more stable by splinting the limb. The best method of doing this is to tie the broken limb to an unbroken and stable part of the body. For leg breaks, this means tying the leg to its unbroken partner using bandages and a substantial layer of padding between the

Splinting a leg

Immobilize an injured lower limb by tying it to the uninjured limb next to it with plenty of soft padding between the two. Check that the bandages are not cutting off the circulation to the limb. Examine the toenails – if they are turning white, the bandages are too tight and require loosening. If the nails turn white when squeezed, but return a red colour when released, circulation is still reaching the end of the limb and the bandages are fine.

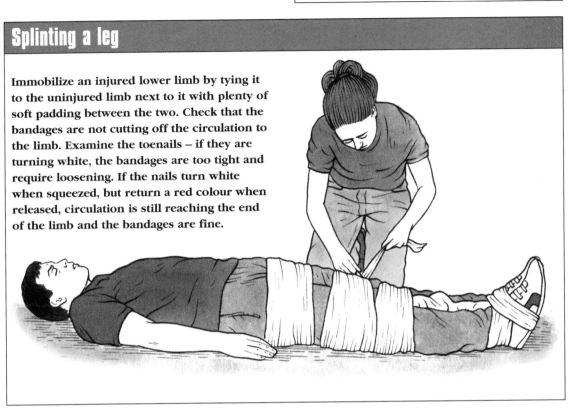

two limbs. For an arm break, place the arm in an improvised sling across the chest. Tie the sling itself to the chest just above the broken limb. If for any reason it is not possible to use an undamaged limb as a splint, use a suitable piece of rigid construction, such as a wooden pole – well padded – as an improvised splint. When splinting a limb, ensure that the bandages are not so tight as to cut off circulation – finger or toe nails should remain pink.

Straightening the limb

A problem with immobilization occurs when the broken limb has formed an irregular angle. If possible, straighten the limb using traction. Gently pull the broken limb in the line of the bone until the limb straightens and can be immobilized. Pull only in a straight line with the bone, and stop if the casualty shows extreme pain when you pull.

Use common sense and follow the rules

A full first-aid training course is required to master the many different permutations of broken bones and dislocated joints, and bandaging is a skill in its own right. But by obeying the common principles of 'steady, support, immobilize' and using common sense you should be able to assist an individual with broken bones until help arrives. As with all first aid, only do what you know is beneficial. Do not attempt treatments if you are unsure of the results.

Serious back injuries

A special category of bone and joint injury is spinal injuries. Spinal injuries are potentially hazardous because of danger to the spinal cord. The spinal cord is a critical element of the nervous system. If severed, pinched, or otherwise damaged, the casualty may be permanently paralysed or even killed instantly.

Moving spinal injury casualties

Spinal injury casualties should not be moved unless absolutely necessary. During movement, the aim is to keep the spine, neck, and head naturally aligned. Here six first aiders work together to roll a spinal injury casualty onto his back. The division of labour should be one person responsible for the head; two for the shoulders, arms, and upper torso; one for the hips; and two for the legs and thighs.

The spinal cord runs down through circular cavities in the vertebra and is normally well protected in its flexible sheath of bone. Danger arises if the vertebra or the intervertebral disks which separate them are driven into the spinal cord. Usually, powerful forces or loads striking the back or neck or twisting the torso abnormally cause such spinal injuries. Serious falls and car accidents are the most common causes of serious back injuries.

If the history of the accident leads you to suspect a spinal injury, you must make a thorough diagnosis. A damaged back is suggested by chronic pain in the back or neck, any unusual deviation in the normal line or contour of the spine, and a sensitivity to gentle touching on the back. If the spinal cord is implicated, the casualty may have no control over the limbs or suffer from numbness or a complete lack of sensation and dexterity in parts of the body; they may also have breathing problems.

Keep the casualty still

Above all else, you must immobilize the casualty in a safe position until the emergency services arrive. Unwarranted movement may aggravate the back or neck injury and threaten the casualty's life. Instruct the casualty not to move. Kneel over his head and support it with your hands. Ideally, the head, and neck, and spine should be aligned. If the head is in a particularly awkward position which is aggravating the injury, cup your hands over the ears and move the head

very slowly until it is in a straight line with the neck and spine. This is known as the 'neutral position'.

Turning over a spinal injury casualty

Support the head and neck further with snugly fitting rolled-up blankets or pieces of clothing. If you have to roll the casualty over onto his front for resuscitation, do so using the 'log-roll' technique. At least four people should assist you. Space the helpers equally along the casualty's body, with one supporting the head in the neutral position. Gently straighten out the casualty's limbs and roll him slowly onto his back. Keep the head in the neutral position throughout the roll, and be particularly conscientious about steadying the legs from the hip to the calf.

HEAD INJURIES AND UNCONSCIOUSNESS

A casualty's level of consciousness often indicates the severity of their injuries. If a casualty is screaming loudly in pain and

Moving a spinal injury casualty

In some circumstances, a spinal injury casualty may to be have moved for his own safety – for example, if he is inside a building that is in danger of collapsing. If this is necessary, first make an improvised collar to brace the head and neck during movement:

- Fold newspaper into a thick rectangle deep enough to fit securely between the casualty's chin and collarbone.
- Wrap the newspaper in a piece of material such as a

scarf, and bend it over your thigh into a U-shape.
- Place the centre of the collar across the front of the casualty's neck, beneath the chin. Ensure that the collar is not pressing on the neck or interfering with breathing.
- Take the loose ends of the material around the back of the neck and tie at the front.
- The collar will provide moderate support and immobilization of the head, although during transit one person should keep holding the head steady. Ideally, a

proper stretcher should be used to carry the casualty, but in an emergency one can be improvised using a blanket.
- The casualty is rolled onto the blanket using the 'log-roll' method (see main text).
- The edges of the blanket are then rolled tightly inwards and used as thick grip edges for the carriers.
- When lifting, there should be equal numbers of people on each side of the stretcher, and one person must give the command for everyone to lift simultaneously.

Estimating percentage of burns coverage

The gravity of a burn varies with what percentage of the body is covered by the injury. Even just 10 per cent of second-degree burns has the potential for volume shock. The same percentage of third-degree burns can easily be fatal. An estimation of how much of the human body is covered by a burn is possible

using the following guidelines:

- Head: 9 per cent
- Front of torso: 18 per cent
- Back of torso: 18 per cent
- Arms: 9 per cent
- Genital area: 1 per cent
- Front of legs: 9 per cent
- Back of legs: 9 per cent
- Feet and hands: 1 per cent for each

shouting demands at you, at least it indicates his breathing, circulation, and nervous system are – for the time being anyway – functioning properly. A silent and unconscious person, however, should be more of an initial concern, as the person's vital functions may be in shutdown – although he also may simply have fainted.

Assessing the casualty

Unconsciousness has many external and internal causes. Internal causes include strokes, heart attacks, shock, epilepsy, fainting, low blood sugar, and even brain tumours. External causes are generally intoxication, poisoning, spinal injuries, and head injuries. All unconscious casualties must first be given an ABC check, and again this should be done at regular intervals to assess any deterioration in vital functions.

Check also for any signs of external bleeding, fractures, or spinal injury, and treat accordingly. Assess the scene for any other indicators of why he is unconscious. Smell the breath for alcohol; examine the arms for syringe marks; check for bracelets or cards that indicate a medical condition such as diabetes or epilepsy. Do not move the casualty or attempt to drag him into a sitting or standing position, and never give him anything to drink.

Check for severity of symptoms

Special precautions are required when dealing with head injuries. Injuries such as concussion – where the brain is shaken by a blow – may result in only a brief period of unconsciousness. When the casualty recovers, his symptoms can include dizziness, nausea, a headache and even loss of memory about the causes of the concussion. If the casualty recovers in less than three minutes he may not require medical attention. Should the headache or nausea persist well after the event the casualty must attend a doctor. In the case of children, any concussion leading to unconsciousness needs professional examination immediately.

Signs of serious injury

More serious head injuries include skull fractures and cerebral compressions. Neither necessarily leads to unconsciousness, but both are potentially fatal. A casualty with a skull fracture will usually display a clear head injury. Look for any wound or contusion, and check for any depressions in the scalp. Examine the eyes for any blood in the white portions. Some very serious fractures may actually distort the symmetry of the face. Clear fluids or watery blood oozing from the nose or ears indicate that cerebrospinal fluid is leaking. A person with a skull fracture may not initially be uncon-scious, but they should be checked constantly for a deteriorating medical condition.

Symptoms may show up later

Cerebral compressions are often associated with skull fractures or other serious head injuries. They consist of a build-up of blood or a swelling within the skull which applies pressure on the brain. The difficulty for the first aider is that the compression may develop hours, even days, after the injury was sustained. A recent head injury is your first clue to cerebral compression. The casualty's mental state will move towards disorientation, drowsiness, and confusion, and his personality may become aggressive or difficult.

Physical symptoms include respiratory difficulty (particularly slow and loud breathing), pupils unequal in size or dilated, rising body temperature, sensations of weakness or paralysis down one side of the body, and finally a lapse into unconsciousness.

Take a suspected casualty to hospital

Both skull fractures and cerebral compressions require immediate and advanced professional medical help. The casualty must be taken to hospital on the merest suspicion of either of these conditions.

For first-aid treatment, lie the casualty down, with the head and shoulders slightly raised. If there is blood loss from the scalp, treat it with the standard procedure for controlling bleeding. Make regular ABC checks, and be prepared to deliver CPR at any moment. If blood or fluids are running out of an ear, turn the casualty's head so that the fluid runs outwards. Dress the ear lightly with a sterile dressing, and keep the wound away from any dirt. Do not plug the ear with material, as this could increase the pressure build-up in the head.

By understanding how to treat wounds, fractures and dislocations, spinal injuries, head injuries, unconsciousness, and respiratory and cardiac failure, you can make the difference between life and death for a casualty. Always remember, however, that your primary goal is to get the casualty to a hospital or doctor. First aid for serious conditions is only a stopgap measure, but it is a crucial one.

Types of bleeding

Bleeding wounds are usually one of five main types:

- Incision – a cut made by a sharp-edged object such as a knife. Incisions can be narrow and inconspicuous, but go deep into the tissue.
- Laceration – a wound made by a force which tears or rips the skin. Lacerations can be awkward injuries to treat because of irregular wound contours and multiple points of bleeding.
- Puncture – a wound resulting from a pointed object being driven into the skin. Puncture wounds to the torso can be particularly serious and implicate major organs.
- Contusion (bruise) – bleeding beneath the skin caused by a blunt-object trauma. Contusions can indicate serious injuries such as fractures and dislocations.
- Abrasion – a scraping injury, usually involving only the surface layers of the skin. Generally non-serious unless involving large body coverage or greater depth of injury.

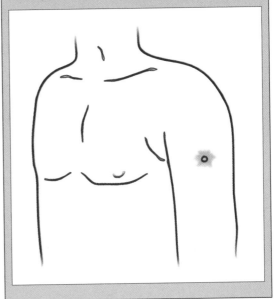

Skin tone and diagnosis

Abnormal coloration in the skin and fingernails can suggest a range of different medical problems and guide you in your diagnosis. For dark-skinned casualties, inspect pale parts of the body – fingernails and toenails, the insides of lips or eyelids, and the soles of the feet.

- **Pale complexion** – this may suggest circulatory shock, especially if the skin is also cool and damp. Other problems include anaemia and malnutrition.
- **Blue or blue/grey** – this hue in the lips and fingernails indicates problems within the circulatory and/or respiratory systems (the colours are the result of a lack of oxygen in the blood).
- **Red** – if accompanied by a disorientated mental condition, this indicates a fever. Red skin, however, can also suggest heat-stroke or simply sunburn in hot climates.
- **Yellow** – generally indicates disease of the liver, such as hepatitis. If this colour is restricted to the face, and with a greenish tinge, this could be an indication of excessive alcohol in the bloodstream.

AVPU CODE

The AVPU code is a common method of assessing the levels of consciousness in a casualty. The results of the assessment guide further treatment and should be relayed to paramedics or doctors.

A = Alert. The casualty is fully consciousness and responsive to their surroundings.

V = Voice. The casualty responds to your voice, although otherwise they may appear unresponsive or confused. Test this level of response by getting the casualty to squeeze your hand or blink their eyes to indicate that they can hear you.

Recovery position

All unconscious casualties should be placed in the recovery position after initial treatment, if the injuries allow this. The position aids the normal processes of breathing, ensures that the tongue does not block the airway, allows unwanted fluids to drain out the mouth, and prevents the casualty choking on his or her own vomit.

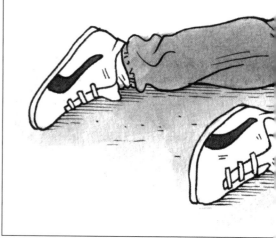

P = Pain. The casualty responds only to pain. Typical medical tests involve scratching the soles of the feet or pinching the earlobes. If the person flinches or pulls away, then the fundamentals of the nervous system are still operating.

U = Unresponsive. The casualty responds to no external stimuli and is completely unconscious.

Check the consciousness of the patient using an AVPU analysis every 10 minutes, and note any improvements or deteriorations in

- Kneel beside the casualty. Tilt the head and chin back to open the airway, straighten the legs, and remove any awkward objects from the casualty's pockets.
- Position the arm nearest to you at a right angle to the body, and lay the other arm across the casualty's chest, with the hand against the opposite cheek.

- Pull the casualty's far leg up just above his other knee and the foot flat on the ground.
- Pull the bent leg over to roll the casualty onto his side, with his head resting on his hand. Tilt the chin so that any fluids drain out. Move the bent leg out to the side at a right angle to prevent the casualty rolling onto his front.

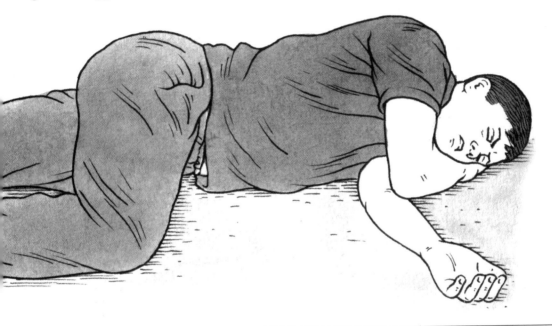

the casualty's condition. Movement down the scale requires additional checking of the casualty's vital signs.

ABSENT LIFE SIGNS

First aid can go a long way to preserving life, but there are distinct limits to what can be achieved. Even highly trained doctors in modern emergency departments are sometimes unable to save very seriously injured people. Learning to spot to signs of death – not always easy to distinguish from a state of unconsciousness – means the living rather than the dead receive your full attention. A dead person will have no respiration or heartbeat. More importantly, his eyes will be fixed and dilated – the pupil does not contract with the introduction of light, signalling brain death. Cover the eyes with your hand for a few seconds, then pull it away to see if the pupils contract. There will be no response to any stimulus – scratch the soles of the feet to check for a response. Try to separate or shield living casualties from the sight of the dead, as it can induce further psychological shock, and focus your mind entirely on helping the living.

Glossary

ABC diagnosis – The initial priorities of a first aid diagnosis: the letters stand for Airway, Breathing, Circulation.

Adrenalin – A hormone released by the adrenal glands, which prepares the body to meet conditions of stress and threat.

Ammonia – Pungent chemical used in fertilizers and household cleaning products, produces toxic, reactive, and corrosive gas capable of causing severe skin, throat and lung burns, high blood pressure, heart attack, and death.

Anthrax – A bacterial disease of sheep and cattle transferable to humans and developed as a biological weapon. Anthrax infection in humans often leads to fatalities, mainly through pneumonia.

AR – Artificial respiration; the process of breathing for a person when their respiration has stopping, using mouth-to-mouth ventilation.

Asphyxiation – Fatal condition occurring when the body is deprived of oxygen by inhaling chemicals such as ammonia, chloroform, carbon monoxide, or carbon dioxide.

AVPU scale – A medical scale used to monitor and judge someone's level of consciousness by describing what they respond to or how responsive they are. It stands for Alert; Voice; Pain; Unconscious.

Barometric detonator – A bomb detonator triggered by changes in atmospheric pressure when the device is taken to different altitudes.

Botulism – A chronic form of food poisoning caused by bacteria growing on unsterilized meats and other foods. Botulism can be cultivated as a biological weapon.

Carbon monoxide – Colorless, odorless, poisonous gas emitted by fuel from cars and heating appliances. Forms carboxyhemoglobin in the lungs, a compound that cuts off oxygen supply to organs and tissues in the body, causing illness and death.

Cerebral compression – A dangerous build-up of pressure on the brain caused by a swelling or bleeding within the skull.

Circulatory shock – A potentially fatal reduction in blood pressure resulting from a loss of body fluid.

CPR – Cardio-pulmonary resuscitation, a first aid treatment for those whose breathing and heart have ceased function. CPR involves alternating between mouth-to-mouth ventilation and chest compressions.

Deadbolt lock – High security lock that automatically bolts together door and frame. It comprises a thick metal cylinder which fits snugly into a mortise or hole in the doorframe.

Dirty bomb – A bomb intended to distribute radioactive material over a wide area.

Fallout – Radioactive particles of dust and debris which descend from the mushroom cloud of a nuclear or atomic explosion.

Flood plain – Drainage area subject to inundation or flooding on a regular annual basis; for example, during seasonal storms when water levels rise.

Focus mitts – Pads worn on the hands and used as targets during punching training.

Ground fault interrupter – Device designed to protect from electrical shock by interrupting a household circuit when a difference occurs in the currents.

Hepatitis – Debilitating viral disease spread by contaminated objects or food supply. Symptoms include jaundice, fatigue, and abdominal pain, loss of appetite, nausea, diarrhoea and fever.

Hurricane straps - Galvanized metal straps that hold a roof down more securely in the event of hurricane force wind.

Hydrofluoric acid - One of the strongest and most corrosive acids, used in some rust removers, water spot stain removers, and vehicle cleaning agents. Causes burns that penetrate deeply into skin and muscle tissue.

Hypothermia - Serious illness caused by dramatic drop in core body temperature leading to damage to muscular and cerebral functions. Usually caused by prolonged exposure to extreme cold accompanied by fatigue, wet clothing, exhaustion, dehydration, and poor food intake.

Incandescent lights - Lights that work by heating up an electrical filament to produce a glow.

Jugular vein - A large vein in the neck carrying blood to the face and neck.

Lake effect snow - Occurs when cold air moves over a body of warmer water, producing condensation and snow. Typically affects Lake Ontario area in the USA and Canada, causing a sudden pile-up of heavy snow.

Larynx - A muscular organ in the neck which provides air passage to the lungs and also contains the vocal cords.

Mercury vapour lights - Mercury vapour gives off ultra violet light when ionized, causing particles inside the light tube to glow or fluoresce.

Motion detonator - A bomb detonator which triggers an explosion when it senses movement.

Phosphoric acid - Clear, colorless, corrosive, odorless liquid used in detergents to produce water softeners, and in fertilizers. At high temperatures forms toxic phosphorus oxides and contact with metals liberates flammable hydrogen gas.

Pressure detonator - A bomb detonator activated by pressure on an external pad or trigger.

Propane - A type of gas used typically in camping stoves and heating equipment.

Pulmonary embolism - Usually fatal condition, commonly caused by deep vein thrombosis, leading to blocked artery in the lungs.

Radiological weapon - A weapon designed to spread harmful radioactive material over a wide area.

Rohypnol - A drug used as a sedative and pre-anaesthetic, also used illegally as a method of sedating an unsuspecting victim prior to robbing or raping them.

Sarin - A lethal nerve gas developed by the Germans during the Second World War.

Smallpox - A contagious viral disease thought to have been eradicated by vaccination in 1976, but now feared as a new-generation biological weapon.

Sodium hydroxide - Also known as caustic soda, or lye, this is a corrosive found in many industrial solvents and cleaners, some drain and oven cleaners. It can react violently with many other substances, including water, and can cause fire or explosion. Reaction with metals releases flammable hydrogen gas.

Strike shield - A large curved pad filled with impact foam. It is held by a training partner and used as a target for punches and kicks.

Sulfuric acid - Extremely corrosive and highly toxic, oily, colorless liquid, also known as vitriol or battery acid. It reacts violently with water and metal.

Telegraphing - In self-defence, telegraphing refers to unconsciousness body signals prior to attack, which indicate the method and moment of assault.

Thermal detonator - A bomb detonator triggered by an increase in surrounding temperature.

Tularaemia - An infectious bacterial disease originating in animals but transferable to humans. It can be produced as a biological weapon.

Typhoid - Life-threatening feverish illness caused by the bacterium Salmonella Typhi, found in sewage water.

Vagus nerves - Cranial nerves supplying the heart, lungs and many other major organs with nervous instruction.

Viral haemorrhagic fevers - Acute viruses producing extensive internal and external bleeding. Some, such as the Ebola virus, are almost 100 per cent lethal.

VX - A lethal nerve gas. Just one milligram of VX on human skin can kill.

Index

M 77239-B
79